Skidboot
The Amazing Dog

Skidboot
The Amazing Dog

Ron Westmoreland
With David Hartwig

EAKIN PRESS 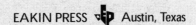 Austin, Texas

All photos are from the Hartwig family collection. Photo on page 133: Tony Barton, Linda Barton (Barbara's sister), Barbara Hartwig, Jay Leno, and David Hartwig, with the star of the show, Skidboot.

FIRST EDITION
Copyright © 2002
By Ron Westmoreland
Published in the United States of America
By Eakin Press
A Division of Sunbelt Media, Inc.
P.O. Drawer 90159 ☐ Austin, Texas 78709-0159
email: sales@eakinpress.com
☐ website: www.eakinpress.com ☐
ALL RIGHTS RESERVED.
1   2   3   4   5   6   7   8   9
1-57168-719-X HB
1-57168-730-0 PB

Library of Congress Cataloging-in-Publication Data
Westmoreland, Ronald P., 1934–
    Skidboot: the amazing dog / by Ron Westmoreland with David
Hartwig–1st ed.
        p.   cm.
    ISBN 1-57168-719-X (HB : alk. paper) – ISBN 1-57168-730-0
(PB : alk. paper)
    1. Skidboot (Dog) 2. Australian cattle dog–Texas–Quinlan. 3.
Hartwig, David, 19455– 4. Dogs–Texas–Quinlan–Biograpny. I.
Hartwig, David, 1955– II. Title.
SF429.A77 W47   2002
636.737–dc21   2002010647

Contents

An Amazing Dog

"Cowboy up" is something every cowboy knows about. Basically it means to do whatever is necessary to get the job done, whether it's riding a bronc while suffering from assorted injuries or going after a bunch of lost cattle in a snow storm.

David Hartwig knows what it is to "cowboy up." He has had both hips replaced and he still shoes horses, competes in calf roping competitions, trains horses, and does ranch work. Other than a little limp sometimes, you would never know he had his hips replaced. He never mentions it.

But even the most casual observer will notice the special bond that exists between David and Skidboot, his amazing dog. I have seen Skidboot accomplish tasks that have left me wondering: "How did he do that?" I've watched Skidboot work cattle, in the same way that other cow dogs work. But I've never seen a cow dog, or any dog, do the things Skidboot does.

I've trained several calf roping horses in the last forty-five years, so that's something I know a bit about. I have never been able to train a dog to do anything other than eat, sleep, and get in the way. One supposed "cow dog" I owned would run in front of my horse when I was roping and trip the horse, causing a heck of a wreck. So, you can see why I'm so amazed at Skidboot's talents.

One evening after David and I had finished roping and were visiting in his living room, I asked how in the world he trained Skidboot to do the tricks he does. He explained that Skidboot does not do tricks. He just does tasks that he's told to do.

"Okay," I said, still confused. I remembered when I gave my kids tasks to do when they were young, and how most of those tasks worked out.

"Can you give me an example?" I asked.

"Okay," David replied, then called Skidboot.

Skidboot walked up and stood there, looking first at David and then at me. Many times I've glanced at Skidboot and noticed that he was staring at my face. I swear he was smiling.

"Skidboot, I want you to go around the kitchen table, tag the chair, pick up your bowl, and take it to the kitchen sink."

I watched carefully for some kind of hand signal or something but didn't see anything other than David standing still beside me.

Skidboot walked to the table and had started around it when David spoke.

"Skidboot, I've changed my mind. Go around the other way."

Skidboot stopped and reversed himself, then walked to the chair and tagged it with his right front foot.

"Skidboot, I've changed my mind again. Tag the chair with your other foot."

Skidboot turned back and tagged the chair with his front left foot.

I was watching Skidboot and David at the same time, and David never made any kind of hand gesture.

Skidboot walked to his bowl, picked it up in his teeth, and laid it ever so gently in the kitchen sink. He returned to David's side and sat looking up at him as if he were thinking, "Okay, that's done. What's next?"

"Good boy, Skidboot," David said, scratching the dog behind the ears.

I thought there must have been something David did that I didn't see.

"How did you teach him that?"

"I didn't teach him. I just asked him to do it, and he did it."

"Yeah, but how did he know how to do it?"

"Well, let's put it this way," David said. "If I told you to go around the table, tag the chair and put the bowl in the sink, could you do it without someone teaching you how to do it?"

"Well, sure. But I'm human! Or at least as human as a cowboy can be . . ."

"I don't know what to tell you. All I have to do is just explain what I want him to do and he does it."

After that day, I never asked again.

I've seen Skidboot do amazing things both in person and on television. When people ask me how he does the things he does, I just shrug my shoulders and reply, "I have no idea."

The only thing I'm sure of is that Skidboot is an amazing dog.

Chapter 1

The Christmas Gift

David Hartwig, with twelve-year-old Russell, eased his pickup to a stop outside a rancher's horse barn in Campbell, Texas. David rolled down the window and peered out at the frost-covered ground.

"I haven't got your mom a Christmas present yet," he remarked more to himself than Russell. "It seems like all I've done is shoe and train horses since last spring. You got any ideas? We better come up with something real quick since this is Christmas Eve. I can't believe I'm shoeing horses on Christmas Eve," he quickly added as he rolled up the window.

Russell wasn't sure if he was supposed to say something or if this was one of those times David just wanted to think out loud. It didn't matter much, because Russell didn't have any ideas either.

"Well, I've got four head to shoe, and sitting here is not going to get it done," David remarked, opening the door and stepping out into the cold.

As both David and Russell fought the wind to get their coats on, Butch Jones walked up.

"Got four head I need you to shoe. You can set up in the barn aisle. That'll get you out of the wind."

"That'll help," David said, sticking out his ungloved hand. "Merry Christmas," he added, and grasped Mr. Jones's cold hand.

"Same to you. Sorry to get you out here on Christmas Eve, but I sure need these horses shod."

"I understand. I'll get it done fast as I can."

After pulling the pickup into the barn, it didn't take long to get all the shoeing tools organized and start on the first horse.

The first horse was a bay gelding with hard, dark-colored hooves. All four shoes were more or less hanging on by a few nails. Usually, David would reset shoes about every six weeks at the longest, but this time it had been at least two months.

David picked up the bay's feet one by one. After placing the horse's foot across his knee, he used nippers to cut off the crimped end of the nail. Then he picked up each foot, holding it between his legs, pulled the nails out, and handed each shoe to Russell. He trimmed the excess hoof growth using long-handled hoof trimmers, and each foot was leveled using a large file or rasp. Now it was time to fit the shoes to each foot and do whatever shaping was required for a good fit. David carefully fitted the shoe and nailed six nails in each foot, three to either side of the shoe. This did not hurt the horse because the hoof wall has no nerve cells—just like a human's fingernails.

After four hours, David had all four horses shod. Then it was time to take a breather.

"Well, that's that," he remarked, as he removed his hat and wiped sweat from his forehead. Sometime between the first and second horse he had shed his coat, and by the fourth horse he was too hot to feel the freezing temperature. He knew he had to put his coat back on or he would have sore muscles in the morning.

"There's a mama dog with a bunch of puppies over there," Russell pointed. "She looks like a blue heeler."

David slipped his shoeing apron off, laid it on the pickup gate, and followed Russell. In an attempt to find a warm spot the mama dog and her pups were huddled in a corner of the drafty barn. It was hard to count how many puppies there were because each one was doing its best to crawl under the other for warmth.

The mama was a basic bluish gray color with black legs and muzzle. She had the characteristics of a blue heeler stock dog, used for decades by stockmen to herd cattle. If a cow slows down or attempts to leave the herd, the heeler will bite at the cow's back legs until it goes forward and returns to the herd. Thus the name "heeler." The term "blue" comes from their color, which is consistently bluish gray. It's been said that one good cow dog is worth three mounted cowboys, especially in rough, brushy country.

"Yep. I believe you're right," David remarked as he studied the pups.

"Mom likes puppies. Maybe one of them would be

a good Christmas present!" Russell said as he picked up a little ball of squirming fur.

"I'll bet she would. That's a good idea," David said, smiling. "I'll see if Mr. Jones wants to sell one."

"I'll do better than that," Mr. Jones said, walking up behind them. "I'll give you the whole bunch. She's a stray that's been around here for about a month or so."

Grinning, David turned and said, "Thanks, but one will do."

"It don't work like that. It's all or nothin'," Mr. Jones replied.

Sometimes it was hard to tell if Mr. Jones was kidding or serious. This time he seemed to be serious.

"I could sure use one as a Christmas present for Barbara. I've messed around and haven't got her one, and I'm about out of time."

Mr. Jones stared down at the squirming puppies for a good while before speaking.

"I'll tell you what . . . since it's for Barbara, you can have your pick of the litter. But soon as I get rid of the rest, you have to take the mama," he said, turning to face David.

"Who's the daddy?" David asked.

"I don't have any idea. Do you want the puppy or not? It's too cold to stand around here looking at a bunch of puppies."

"Okay, we'll take one," David said, turning to a smiling Russell. "Which one should we get?"

Russell picked the pups up one at a time until he and David decided on a fat little bundle of white.

"This one okay with you?" David asked Mr. Jones.

"I told you I wanted you to take 'em all, so why would I care which one you take?"

With that said, Mr. Jones handed David a check for the horseshoeing and started toward his house.

"Hey, you didn't pay me to take this puppy. It ought to be worth something to get rid of it," David called out, smiling.

"It's best you get out of here before I change my mind and make you take 'em all."

Russell held the new puppy close to keep him warm as they drove home.

They hadn't gone far when David pulled over to the side of the road. "What if we didn't get the best pup?" he asked, more to himself than Russell.

A little confused, Russell glanced at the puppy and then at David. "How would you know which one was the best?" he asked.

"I'm not sure, but we should have paid more attention to them. I don't know if he can see or hear or whatever."

David continued driving for a few miles while he thought more about it.

"Well . . . I think we better go back for another look," David said, as he made a U-turn.

When they pulled in the driveway, Mr. Jones came out of his house. "What now?" he asked.

"We want to take another look at the pups. We might want to change," David called out.

"Do whatever you want . . . I'm going inside by the fire," Mr. Jones called out as he shut the door.

As they approached the puppies, one stood off a few feet from the others. He was alert and watched them carefully as they approached. He didn't move, even when Russell returned the fat puppy to his mother.

"What do you think about that pup?" David asked, pointing at the little standoff puppy.

"He's an independent little rascal," Russell observed.

"He sure is, and he's a male."

"He kind of looks like a 'possum with that grayish colored fur," Russell said, walking toward the puppy.

Grrrr . . . keep your distance. I don't know who or what you are, but don't mess with me.

Russell walked closer and bent over to pick up the growling puppy.

"The little rascal thinks he's tough," Russell said, smiling.

Grrrrr . . . better leave me alone, you big two-legged whatchamacallit.

"Better be careful, Russell . . . he acts pretty ferocious," a grinning David called out.

Russell had to trap the pup by herding him next to the barn wall then grabbing him as he ran by.

"That little rascal is something else. Did you see how strong and fast he is?" Russell held the squirming pup.

"Yeah, I believe he's the one."

Let me go . . . or I'll make you wish that you had . . .

Russell jerked his hand back from around the puppy. "That little rascal bit me!"

David laughed. "He's got spunk! He'll make a good'un. Don't let him eat you up."

"I wonder how him and Fred will get along?" Russell asked.

"I imagine Fred will let him know who's boss pretty quick."

"How do you think dogs learn how to do things?"

"Well, that's a good question. I believe they learn from watching what other dogs do and how they're treated by people. And, I think a lot is bred in them. They just do things instinctively. Take cow dogs, for example. It's just bred in 'em to herd cattle. And a bird dog instinctively smells out birds and points at them."

"Well . . . I hope this pup don't learn too much from Fred," Russell added.

That remark brought a quick smile to David as he remembered the many times he spent driving the countryside in an attempt to locate a roving Fred. "Yeah, there's some things best not learned. I imagine he'll find enough trouble to get into without any help from Fred." He opened the truck door. "One thing we have to do is name him before we get home. If we don't, there's no telling what your mom will name him."

They drove for several miles before either of them spoke.

"We need to name him something about cowboying or roping," David said, turning to Russell.

"How about Barbed Wire?" Russell said.

"Hmm . . . How about Catch Rope?" David countered.

"What about Boots?"

"Yeah . . . how about Piggin' String? Nope, there's a bunch of dogs named Piggin' String," David muttered, more to himself than to Russell. He glanced first at the pup squirming in Russell's lap, then at Russell. "Hey, how about Skidboot?"

David reminded Russell that skidboots are the padded leather boots attached to the back ankles of calf-roping horses. They are designed to keep the horse from being injured when sliding or "skidding" to a stop. The boots are tough—just like this little dog seemed to be.

"I like it!" Russell answered, looking down at the pup. "Hey, Skidboot, how do you like your name?"

Skidboot? What kind of name is that? My name should be something that fits me, like Mad Dog, or Blue Thunder. Anything but Skidboot! But I guess it's better than Sylvester . . .

"I think he likes it," Russell said, rubbing Skidboot's head and ears.

Knock it off, buster! When I want to be petted I'll let you know when.

"The little rascal growled at me again!" Russell laughed.

As they pulled in the driveway, David turned to

Russell. "I'm going to fool your mom, so don't say anything about the puppy."

David reached for Skidboot, and as he did, Skidboot growled.

Grrrrr . . . don't mess with me, Too Tall. I'll give you some of the same I gave the shorter one.

David stuck Skidboot inside his coat, where the pup could barely get his head out. Just as he reached the front steps David zipped his coat, and Barbara opened the door.

"I was starting to worry," she said, pushing the door open.

David put on his most pained expression. "A horse kicked me right here," he motioned to his chest.

"How bad is it?"

"I'll show you." David unzipped his coat, and a furry head popped out.

Barbara was stunned for a moment, then reached out to grab the squirming Skidboot.

Hey . . . what's going on? Quit passing me around! This is no way to get on my good side.

"He's a little bundle of fur," Barbara said, running her fingers through Skidboot's hair.

"Merry Christmas," David said, as he hugged Barbara.

Chapter 2
The Trouble Begins

On Christmas morning in the Hartwig household, not a creature was stirring—that is, except for an inquisitive Skidboot. He had already found that Russell's blanket was softer and warmer than the old rug put down in the corner for him to sleep on. He pulled and pulled until he freed the blanket from Russell's grasp, and after a lot of scratching and fluffing he got it just the way he wanted it.

After all that work, he was hungry. Earlier he had roamed through the house trying to find his mom, without success. He had eaten the puppy chow and spilled the milk Barbara left for him, and his searching had not resulted in anything else worth eating. The strange tree and all the packages under it looked promising. But, after tearing them open, he found nothing worth eating, though he tried. He gave up and returned to Russell's blanket.

Half awake, David staggered into the den. He

glanced toward the Christmas tree as he passed it en route to the coffee pot. He abruptly stopped and turned around to take another look at the tree and presents. The full impact of what his blurry eyes told him he was seeing hit him. Wrapping paper and presents were scattered from one end of the den to the other. The Christmas tree, minus most of the decorations, was leaning against the wall.

"What the ... Barbara, come here please!" he shouted.

A sleepy Barbara leaned against the hall doorway. "What is it?" she asked, rubbing her eyes.

"Look what your dog did."

"Oh my goodness," she said, as she witnessed the full impact of the devastation before her.

"Where's that worthless dog?" David asked, as he began searching.

"Check Russell's room."

David opened Russell's bedroom door to find Skidboot curled up in Russell's blanket on the floor.

"Here he is!" David shouted.

The shouting woke both Russell and Skidboot.

"What's wrong?" Russell asked.

"Go take a look in the den," David said, staring at Skidboot.

The puppy, still snuggled up in Russell's blanket, looked up at David.

Now what, Too Tall?

David was still staring at Skidboot when Barbara walked in.

"Remember, David, he's just a puppy."

"Yeah, I'm trying to remember."

They decided since it was Christmas Day there was no reason to rewrap presents, so they just sorted and handed them out. More than a few had small tooth marks as a bonus.

"Merry Christmas, Barbara," David said, pointing at Skidboot, who was watching with interest.

Hey, I hope y'all can find something to eat in all that stuff! I couldn't . . .

After the Christmas disaster, Skidboot sensed that maybe he did something he wasn't supposed to have done. Russell and Barbara seemed to forgive him. After all, he was just a puppy, they would say. But with

David, it was altogether different. He avoided Skidboot. It was apparent it would be up to Russell and Barbara to take care of him.

With Barbara working and Russell going to school, there were some things David had to do for Skidboot, but he did them grudgingly.

Then things got even worse for David. Mr. Jones drove up one morning and unloaded Skidboot's mother.

As David walked up to the truck, Mr. Jones turned and said, "Brought your dog."

"Not *my* dog. I've got more dogs than I need now," David responded, offering his hand.

"You forgetting our deal Christmas Eve?" he asked, shaking David's hand.

"I was hoping you had."

"Not likely."

They stood watching the dog as she sniffed the air.

"Smells the other dogs, I guess."

"She's a lot thinner than I remember."

"If you'd nursed seven half-grown dogs you'd be thin, too."

As they stood watching, Fred, Russell's dog, eased from around the house and walked up to smell the blue heeler.

"Are we going to see a fight?" Mr. Jones asked, backing toward his truck.

"Not likely. Fred's a lover, not a fighter. He's never found any reason to fight anything."

"He's a mixed Border collie, isn't he?"

"Yep."

"Will he work cattle?" Mr. Jones asked, still watching the dogs.

"Nope. Fred mostly likes to eat, sleep, get petted, and do whatever he wants."

"Kind of sounds like my kids," Mr. Jones remarked. "Well, got to go. I'll need my horses shod again right away, so I figure you'll do it for nothin' since I gave you this good dog."

"You need to pay *me* for taking her off your hands.

I still don't remember saying anything about taking her," David replied, smiling.

As Mr. Jones drove off, David looked down at the mother dog and Fred staring up at him.

"Oh man, what have I done?"

After some amount of discussion, and over David's objection, Skidboot's mother was named Blue Bell. David told them not to get attached to her. She wouldn't be there long.

Skidboot recognized his mother and attempted to pick up where he left off. However, Blue Bell was not having any of it. Skidboot was a big boy now and had to act like one, and that meant no nursing. After getting snapped at a few times, Skidboot gave it up as a lost cause.

After that rude awakening, he decided to be Fred's pal.

On warm days, when it wasn't raining, David would let Skidboot follow him around while he fed and cared for the livestock. On one particular day, Skidboot had even more energy than usual. He was looking for something to chase or fight.

After a midafternoon nap, Fred eased out to where David was pouring feed in the calves' feed trough.

Easing and sleeping were two things Fred took pride in. Anything associated with exercise was something to be avoided. Work was something he saw no need in. Just the thought of it made him shudder.

Skidboot saw Fred coming and ran to greet his new-found buddy.

Hey, Fred, you want to play?

Get lost, Shorty.

Ignoring Fred's gruff manner, Skidboot leaped across Fred's back and bit at his ears. Fred turned and almost put Skidboot's whole head in his mouth, just to let him know who was the boss.

Skidboot backed away and stood shaking his head.

Hey, what's the deal?

Young 'un, you got to learn respect for your elders. You do what I want you to do when I want you to do it. You got it?

Skidboot had never been treated so badly before. Oh, David shouted at him all the time, but he just ignored that.

After being scolded by Fred, he decided to look elsewhere for companionship. He saw Blue Bell lying on the front porch, so he ran to her and began crawling all over her and biting at her ears.

That's enough, Skidboot. Go bother Fred.

Fred's in a bad mood . . .

Well, go away. I'm tired and I need a nap. I heard noises all night and spent most of the evening checking around the barn for varmints.

A dejected Skidboot slowly walked back to the barn, where David was finishing up with the feeding. As he turned the fence corner, he saw a calf heading for the feed trough. Skidboot took off running toward him.

"Skidboot, leave that calf alone!" David yelled.

Skidboot was right on the calf's heels, biting and growling.

Blue Thunder's after you now, calf! You got no place to hide! You belong to me!

"Dang it, Skidboot, leave that calf alone!" David yelled once more as he picked up a stick and waved it at Skidboot.

I can't hear you, Too Tall. You might as well be blowing smoke. This calf is mine and mine alone. I'm the boss of this herd.

About the time Skidboot was about to run the calf through the fence, David threw the stick at him.

Well . . . it's about time someone decided to play with me!

Skidboot forgot about the calf and ran for the stick, which had fallen far short of the intended target. He quickly picked it up in his mouth and began to shake it. Then, seeing that David wasn't chasing after him, he turned and ran by him, stick in mouth.

Grrrr . . . Grrrr . . . Come and get it, Too Tall, if you can.

David watched as Skidboot shook the stick so violently that he threw himself down.

"Crazy dog," David mumbled to himself. He grabbed the empty feed sacks and headed back to the house.

Chapter 3
Demon Dog

By spring, David was spending more and more time training and shoeing horses, and Skidboot was getting into more and more trouble. He was called "The Demon Dog" as often as he was "Skidboot." He didn't obey Barbara and Russell any more than he did David. But with David, it seemed as if he took pleasure in agitating him. Because Barbara and Russell were gone during the day, Skidboot, a.k.a. "The Demon Dog," became David's responsibility, and that didn't help matters.

Skidboot had shed most of his puppy hair and was now showing his mother's bluish gray color. He was getting taller every day. And his attitude seemed to grow—worse—as well.

Every day of his life now, David regretted the day he brought the puppy home. If it wasn't for Barbara he would have already hauled him off.

If David let him outside, Skidboot would chase the horses and calves, and no amount of yelling would stop

him. Whenever David was calf roping, Skidboot would dart into the roping pen and chase after either the calf or the horse David was riding. David would have to stop roping, tie up his horse, and attempt to catch Skidboot. The dog wouldn't come when called, and was impossible to catch. After David would run him off, Skidboot would just sneak back. Then it was all to do over. It seemed he was intentionally doing this to aggravate David.

Locking him in the house alone was a disaster. He would chew on table legs, pull and tear at the furniture—anything to cause trouble.

One warm, sunny morning, David had several head of horses to shoe, and he sure didn't want or need any trouble from Skidboot. So, before letting Skidboot outside, David kneeled down beside the independent pup, grabbed him by the scruff of his neck, and softly but firmly said:

"Listen, dog, I'm goin' to let you outside. I don't want you chasing the stock or bothering me. If you do, you're going to lose a good home. Do you understand?" David looked Skidboot eye to eye.

Grrrr . . . get your hand off me, or I'll bite you again!

"Don't you bite me," David said sternly.

Then get your hands off me and open the door. Your threats don't bother Blue Thunder. I've got the boss and Russell on my side. So, let's get on with the show . . .

David went to the barn and Skidboot went investigating.

The first thing that got his attention was Fred curled up next to the sunny side of the barn.

Hey ... wake up!

Fred opened his eyes, then closed them.

Go away, Shorty. Go bother Blue Bell, or whoever ...

Come on, Fred, let's do something. There's cattle to chase, and we can bother Too Tall, if nothing else.

Something had to be done about this pest, Fred thought. Then he had an idea. What if he got Shorty to follow him, then after he got him lost, he would run off and leave him? No one would miss him. Well, maybe Barbara and Russell. But they'd get over it soon enough.

Okay, Shorty, let's investigate. There's some great places down in the bottoms, and we might even find a deer or two you can chase.

Skidboot's eyes lit up, and he began to run circles around Fred as he eased toward the bottom land.

What's a deer?

A deer is kind of like a calf, but different. You'll see soon enough.

Fred thought maybe things would get back to normal around the ranch with Skidboot gone. Everyone seemed to be in a bad mood most of the time.

David came out of the barn leading a horse and saw Fred and Skidboot ducking under the fence, heading for the bottom land. He whistled and shouted at the dogs, but neither slowed down or looked back.

"Fred! Skidboot! Come here, boys," David pleaded.

Too Tall's yelling again.

Don't look back. Just act like you don't hear him. I've been doing this for years. He'll finally give up.

They were far into the woods before they saw the first deer.

There's a deer . . . go get him!

Skidboot took off in a hard run just as the deer saw him. The deer was jumping fallen trees and brush piles that Skidboot had to quickly find a way to get around. But he was still where he could see the deer. He was still in the hunt.

Wow, deer sure are faster than calves!

Then the deer was gone. Skidboot turned around, expecting to see Fred. But he was nowhere to be seen. He walked one direction, then the other. Nothing looked familiar. Then it hit him: He was lost.

After seeing that Skidboot was well out of sight, Fred chuckled, then headed back to the ranch in a good ground-covering trot. He was proud of himself.

Well, that's that . . .

Skidboot had no idea which way was home. He figured the best thing to do was find Fred.

After what seemed like hours, he was getting tired and thirsty. He came across the river and decided that would be a good place to rest and get a drink. He had never drunk water from any place other than his water bowl.

This stuff not only stinks, it tastes like mud.

He wrinkled up his nose at the thought, but he had to have liquid to survive.

Back at home, David saw Fred trying to sneak into the barn. But he didn't see Skidboot anywhere.

"Fred, here boy," David called.

True to form, Fred ignored him.

Oh, great, he saw me. Now what? Best thing to do is just play dumb.

David walked into the barn and saw Fred curled up in a corner doing his best impression of sleeping.

"Where's Skidboot? I know you and him went off together."

David spent so much time alone with animals, he had started talking to them as if they were human. He stood looking down at Fred with his hands on his hips. Fred looked up with one of his best sincere looks.

I'll never tell . . .

David walked outside and looked toward the bottom land. That was the last place he had seen Skidboot. After pausing for a few minutes and shouting Skidboot's name, he decided to saddle a horse and go look for him.

Not knowing exactly what to expect, David caught an older gelding called Gray Ghost. He was gentle, but, even more important, he was dependable. Nothing excited him.

It was midafternoon by the time he rode into the

wooded area of the bottom land. This area was subject to flooding, but at that time it was only muddy. The river was well within its banks.

It was hard to cover a lot of distance because of mud bogs, brush piles, and fallen trees. After a couple of hours, David decided to tie Gray Ghost and look on foot. He thrashed through brush and tripped and fell at least half a dozen times before he noticed movement off to the side.

"Skidboot . . . Here, boy!" he shouted and whistled. Skidboot heard the familiar voice. He ran toward it.

Hey, are you lost, too?

David heard Skidboot before he could actually see him through the tall underbrush.

"Well, another wasted day. Can't you manage to stay out of trouble for one day?" David said, as Skidboot looked up at him.

Yeah, I'm all right. Thanks for asking.

"If it wasn't for Barbara, I'd just as soon leave you here," David scolded.

Other than being covered in mud and matted with sandburs, Skidboot was no worse for wear.

David walked back to where he had tied the horse. Skidboot trailed behind him at a respectable distance. He didn't want David to think he was helping him.

David mounted Gray Ghost and began the long ride home with Skidboot following.

Where's Fred?

Skidboot stopped and looked back in the direction they had come from.

David reined Gray to a stop when he noticed Skidboot wasn't following.

"Come on, dog. It's going to be dark soon. I don't want to cripple a good horse on account of you," David shouted, and turned around in the saddle in an attempt to find Skidboot.

Skidboot heard David call, but, as Fred had taught, ignored him.

David rode back to where Skidboot was standing with his nose held high, sniffing.

"Come on, dog, enough is enough. I'll drag you home if I have to! Come on!"

After sniffing the wind for any scent of Fred and not smelling anything but river mud, Skidboot finally gave up and followed along behind Gray.

All the way back to the ranch, Skidboot worried about what had happened to Fred. He felt he had abandoned his friend.

The sun was just setting on the western horizon as they approached the barn lot.

As David unsaddled the horse and fed him, a dejected

Skidboot slowly walked toward the ranch house. As he got closer, he saw Fred sleeping on the front porch. Forgetting how tired he was, he ran up to Fred, waking him from his nap.

Hey, Fred, I thought you were lost!

Skidboot began licking him in the face.

Oh great, I can't win.

Fred stood up in an attempt to get away from Skidboot's enthusiasm.

Barbara and Russell pulled into the driveway just as David walked up. Noticing Skidboot's matted, mud-covered coat, Barbara looked at David. "What happened to him?" she asked.

Sensing that Barbara was concerned, Skidboot put on his "I'm really in bad shape" act. He hunkered down and almost crawled to Barbara, looking up at her with his best "poor dog" look.

"Poor little Skidboot, what happened to you?" Barbara asked as she bent down to pet him.

Skidboot glanced toward David, who couldn't believe what he was seeing.

What an actor, David thought.

Eat your heart out, Too Tall. Me and the boss are tight.

After spending a good hour with Skidboot in the bath tub, Barbara finally scrubbed and pulled the sand-burs and mud off. Giving himself a good shaking, the exhausted Skidboot curled up on Russell's bed and went to sleep.

David told Barbara about Fred and Skidboot going to the bottom and how he had to find and bring him home. They both agreed that maybe Fred did it on purpose. He didn't like anyone or anything disturbing his life. He liked things just the way they were before Skidboot and Blue Bell came.

Meanwhile, outside, a dejected Fred eased out to the barn, where Blue Bell stood watching as he approached. Blue Bell was aggravated at Fred.

You did that on purpose . . .

Give me a break. I'm not in the mood . . .

Fred found a pile of feed sacks in the tack room, and after fluffing them up just the way he wanted, he lay down. He fell fast asleep as Blue Bell continued to admonish him for attempting to lose Skidboot.

Chapter 4
Disaster Strikes

By the next morning Skidboot was back to his old reckless self. As soon as David let him outside, he immediately searched for Fred, but couldn't locate him anywhere. So he looked for Blue Bell.

He finally found Blue Bell in the tack room, and, much to his surprise, she had a litter of puppies.

Skidboot stopped in his tracks and stared at the small little things as they squirmed to get up under their mother. Blue Bell, like a good mother, gently nudged each puppy next to her so they could nurse.

Skidboot was stunned beyond belief. All he could do was just stare.

Wow . . . wow . . . Where did all those puppies come from?

Blue Bell glanced up at Skidboot when he walked into the tack room and watched his reaction to her young brood.

These are your brothers and sisters, Skidboot. You're a big brother now.

I'm what? To who? Why?

I'll explain it all to you, but right now I'm too tired.

With that said, Blue Bell laid her head down and closed her eyes.

Hey, why are their eyes shut?

Blue Bell opened her eyes, and thought that maybe Fred was right about one thing: Skidboot was a pest.

They can't see, at least for a while. Now, go play with Fred or something. I've got to rest.

But . . .

Go away, now . . .

Blue Bell closed her eyes once more as Skidboot continued to stare at the puppies snuggled next to their mother. The memory of snuggling next to her was a distant one, but one that still tugged at him.

Not one to dwell on the past, after one more glance at Blue Bell and the puppies Skidboot left in search of Fred and something to get into. There were calves and horses to chase, but, at least for now, he thought he'd stay away from chasing deer.

Fred had been coming around the side of the house just as Skidboot approached the tack room to visit Blue Bell. After seeing Skidboot go into the barn, Fred had ducked under the house, positioning himself so he could see the barn but where he couldn't be seen.

Skidboot went to all of Fred's hangouts, but couldn't find the elusive Border collie. Going back to the house for one more look, he saw David roping in the arena. As if in a trance, he started toward the arena, first at a walk, then, as if he had been directed by some unseen

master, he took off in a run straight for the arena. He ducked under the fence just as the calf ran by and gave chase.

David saw Skidboot as he ducked under the fence. He reared back on the reins and slid his roping horse to a stop a split second before he ran over Skidboot.

"You numbskull. You just about got yourself killed and me, too!" David shouted, as he watched Skidboot chase the calf into the catch pen.

Skidboot walked out of the catch pen into the arena, feeling pretty good about himself.

Now, that's the way to pen a calf, Too Tall. Blue Thunder rules!

If he had been able, he would have patted himself on the back.

No need to thank me, it's all in a day's work for a cow dog.

Skidboot stood facing David, waiting for praise for a job well done.

"I've got to do something about you before you get your fool self killed, or cripple a horse, or even worse, cripple me. If you get hurt or killed, Barbara will never forgive me," David said, frowning at Skidboot.

What is your problem, Too Tall? You were chasing the calf to the catch pen and all I did was kinda speed him along. Oh well, I've got better things to do anyhow.

Skidboot turned and headed toward the house to look for Fred.

Meanwhile, Fred had watched the whole thing unfold from his vantage point under the house.

Here he comes. I'll just wait him out.

Skidboot checked all of Fred's favorite relaxing spots but couldn't find him. He decided to check the front porch one last time. He walked up on the porch, then walked around the house, but no Fred. He was about to give up when he glanced at an opening under the house and saw Fred's tail.

Thinking he was playing hide and seek, which it seemed like Fred played a lot, Skidboot ducked through the opening and leaped on top of Fred.

I found you, now you're it!

Skidboot bit at Fred's ears and licked him in the face. To say he was excited would be an understatement. A dejected Fred got to his feet and walked out from under the house.

Wonderful, this is just great . . .

Blue Bell has a bunch of puppies! Come on, I'll show you.

What? No way. This can't be happening to me. There's already too many dogs around here now, and there's going to be more. How much more can I take?

Fred couldn't believe it, but there they were—five little bundles of future trouble.

Skidboot stood at the tack room door, beaming with pride. He had brothers and sisters. He didn't remember his other brothers and sisters from his litter, no matter how hard he tried. But this time he would.

As Fred watched the puppies nursing, he glanced at Blue Bell. She seemed content, so maybe it wasn't all bad.

Fred decided the best thing to do right then was to put some distance between him, Skidboot, Blue Bell, and her puppies. So he headed down the ranch house lane toward the highway.

He hadn't gone far when he saw Skidboot running to catch up with him.

Oh, great. There's no peace from him.

Hey, Fred, wait up . . .

Fred started to trot, but he knew there was no way he could outdistance Skidboot. He settled back to his usual slow pace.

After reaching Fred, Skidboot went on and on about the puppies and what he was going to teach them when they got older.

Okay, motor mouth, give me a break.

Meanwhile, David had been busy feeding the livestock. He had several horses he needed to work with, and with a rodeo coming up he needed to practice roping and tying. It seemed that shoeing, caring for the livestock, and doing a little horse training didn't leave any time for roping practice.

He didn't know about Blue Bell's puppies until he went into the tack room to saddle a horse.

"Well, Blue Bell, what do we have here?" David remarked as he bent down to see the puppies. He examined them one at a time until he was satisfied they appeared to be healthy.

As he stood watching the puppies trying to position themselves to nurse, he thought about Skidboot. He tried to remember the last time he saw him. *It was when I ran him off,* he thought, and he walked to the barn door.

"Skidboot . . . here, boy!" he shouted and whistled. Uh-oh, Fred's not here either, he realized.

Fred and Skidboot had covered at least two miles across pastures and two county roads, and Fred was getting tired.

What I'm trying to get away from is right here with me. Why am I wearing myself out?

Fred found a shade tree close to a green pasture and lay down.

Skidboot was still raring to go and stood looking down at Fred, who by now was enjoying a nap. After a few minutes of watching Fred sleep, Skidboot looked around for something to do. He spotted the biggest black calf he had ever seen grazing in the pasture. The urge to chase got the best of him, and he started toward the calf.

What Skidboot didn't know was that the big black calf was a Brangus bull that weighed around twelve hundred pounds. Also, he didn't know that a bull this size could be dangerous.

At first the bull didn't notice Skidboot. As Skidboot got closer, the bull raised his massive head.

Skidboot accelerated and attempted to position himself at the bull's rear. Running at the bull's back feet, he barked and attempted to bite the feet. But the bull was too fast. He turned and faced Skidboot. Head down, the bull snorted and pawed the ground.

Now, this was different from running David's roping calves. Those calves would run when he went after them. Also, this calf was ten times bigger.

Hey, you're supposed to run and I'm supposed to chase you.

It was a standoff. Skidboot stood not more than ten feet away from the bull with his head down while the bull snorted and pawed the ground, intently watching Skidboot.

Fred, aroused from his nap by all the snorting, glanced up to see the standoff in progress.

Great . . . I just wanted him gone, not dead. Now what? There's no way I'm going in there. The kid's on his own.

Fred eased closer to the pasture fence. Maybe he could distract the bull by barking, giving Skidboot a chance to escape.

Woof . . . woof . . . Get out of there, kid, before you get yourself killed!

No response from either Skidboot or the bull. They both continued to stare each other down.

With a sick feeling, Fred ducked under the fence. He was about halfway from the fence line and the standoff when Skidboot saw him coming. Skidboot suddenly felt confident. Between the two of them, they could handle this big calf, he thought. He lunged toward the bull, who didn't turn and run like David's roping calves. Instead, he lowered his head and charged Skidboot.

Uh-oh, time to go!

Fred quickly turned and ducked back under the fence.

Faster than Skidboot could react, the bull was on top of him. In an attempt to kick or step on Skidboot, the bull managed to land a solid blow with a hard-driven back foot, sending Skidboot flying.

As Skidboot attempted to gain his footing and stand up, the bull stood close by, snorting and pawing the ground.

Wow . . . that's one mean calf.

As he slowly stood up, Skidboot felt a sharp pain in his leg. Glancing down, he saw blood oozing from a gash.

Oh boy, this is not good.

Then he glanced up at the bull, who was still very, very upset.

Woof . . . woof . . . Get the heck out of there!

Fred was doing what he could on the other side of the fence.

Skidboot glanced up at the bull, then at his bleeding leg, and decided maybe Fred was right. Maybe this calf was just too big and mean. He got to his feet and limped over to where Fred was standing.

Look, Shorty, before you go off half-cocked, you'd better know what you're doing. That bull could have you and half a dozen like you for breakfast! There's a lot of difference between a calf and a grown bull.

Skidboot looked at his bleeding leg.

Yeah, I'm finding that out.

By the time they were almost home, Skidboot was hurting. He could barely limp along.

David had been frantically searching for Skidboot and Fred. He knew if he found one the other wouldn't be far away. He had ridden down to the bottom without success, and was just about ready to take the truck and check toward the highway when he saw Fred and Skidboot cutting across the pasture.

Oh great ... there's David. I'll bet I get the blame again.

As Fred headed toward the security of the barn, Skidboot limped up to the porch.

David noticed Skidboot limping and went to check on him. Every time he touched his foot or leg, Skidboot would growl and bare his teeth.

Grrr ... Grrr ... Leave me alone.

David could tell the wound required stitches. After a lot of growling, David finally picked up Skidboot and placed him in the front seat. He was almost to the highway when he met Barbara coming home from work. He pulled over and waited until they were side by side.

"What's wrong?" Barbara asked, after seeing David's somber face.

"Skidboot got kicked by a horse or a cow on the foot and leg. He needs stitching up."

"Put him in my truck. I'll take him to the veterinarian. I know you've got things to do at home."

David picked up Skidboot and laid him down on the front seat of Barbara's truck.

"Bless your heart, Skidboot," Barbara said, looking down at the wound.

Yeah, you don't know the half of it. It's worse than it looks.

Skidboot looked up at Barbara with his best pitiful look.

It took ten stitches to close the wounds. Skidboot tried to be brave, but it was hard. Barbara held him close to her throughout the whole ordeal, so it wasn't all that bad. The worst part was when the vet came at him with a needle.

Uh-oh, I don't like the looks of this.

The closer the vet got, the closer Skidboot got to Barbara.

Grrr . . . grrr . . . don't touch me or I'll bite you!

"It's all right, Skidboot, it won't hurt," Barbara assured.

Oh yeah, easy for you to say. You're not the one that's going to get run through.

On the way home Skidboot couldn't get close enough to Barbara. If it hadn't been for the steering wheel, he would have crawled into her lap. He took the poor, hurt dog routine to new heights. He would look up at Barbara with eyes half closed and whimper.

Take care of me . . . I'm hurt bad.

When they passed where the bull was grazing, Skidboot stood up and growled.

I'll get you for this! No one wrongs Blue Thunder and gets away with it. I shall return!

For the next several days Skidboot lazed around the house, enjoying being babied by Barbara and Russell. It was something he could get used to.

Fred decided it would be best to keep a low profile. Finding ways of getting rid of Skidboot were becoming harder and riskier. The young dog was like a cat with nine lives.

David managed to get a lot done around the ranch without Skidboot's constant interference. For at least a while, things were pretty quiet around the ranch. But with Skidboot around, it wouldn't stay that way long.

Chapter 5
Trouble Grows

It was early fall, and Skidboot had made a complete recovery. He was back to acting like his old self. By now he had worn out his welcome at the house, and even Barbara was beginning to lose patience with his antics.

Left unattended, he once again pulled all the cover from the beds, chewed table legs to the point it appeared beavers had been in the house, and generally played havoc with everything and everybody.

When turned outside, he continually chased horses and calves. Even Blue Bell hated to see him coming. David gave up on scolding him and had resorted to throwing whatever he could find at him, but nothing worked. Fred began leaving before Skidboot was let outside in the morning and stayed gone all day.

Finally, David had had enough.

I'm going to talk to Barbara about this dog. Something has to be done. He's making everyone's life a

living nightmare, David thought as he finished shoeing a horse. He had to stop shoeing several times to yell at Skidboot for chasing calves. Out of frustration, he threw a stick at him. Thinking it was a game, Skidboot ran off with the stick, but lost interest when David didn't chase him.

Skidboot searched for Fred in all his old hiding places but couldn't find him anywhere. Blue Bell even growled at him when he attempted to get the puppies to play with him.

Dejected, he slowly walked up the lane toward the county road.

Man, what a drag. All Too Tall does is yell and carry on, which is no more than I expect. But even Barbara and Russell are avoiding me. My own mother don't want me around, and Fred must have left the ranch completely.

He was careful to avoid the black bull. He stood a safe distance outside the pasture fence, watching him graze.

Yeah, you big black devil. You'd like for me to come in there so you could get another shot at me. But it ain't goin' to happen.

He was almost to the county road when he noticed Fred lying under a tree. As he got closer, he could tell Fred was fast asleep. This was too good to pass up.

Easing up next to Fred, Skidboot reared back and jumped to straddle Fred's back.

Yelp, yelp . . . What's happening?

Fred leaped to his feet in order to dislodge the attacker. Skidboot held on for a couple of violent shakes, then fell to the ground.

Got you that time!

Grrrr ... That's it, I can't take it anymore.

Fred leaped for Skidboot. Grabbing him by the loose skin on his shoulder, he shook him violently.

Hey, what's the deal? No reason to get all upset. I'm just glad to see you.

After getting over the initial shock of the rude awakening, Fred released his grip on Skidboot and stood over him, growling.

You ever do something like that again it will be your last. Got it?

Yeah, yeah, I got it. Why are you so sore?

Forget it, you wouldn't understand.

Attempting to ignore him, Fred decided he might as well go home since the reason he had left once again was standing next to him.

All the way home, neither talked. All Fred could think about was how he could get rid of Skidboot, and Skidboot was looking around for something to get into.

That night, David approached Barbara about Skidboot.

"We've got to talk about Skidboot," David said.

"Okay, talk."

"He's getting worse. We can't leave him in the

house, and when we let him outside he chases the livestock. Then to make matters even worse, you can't call
him. He won't mind at all. I'm at the end of my rope."

"I don't have an answer. But, you're right, something has to be done."

"I suppose I could find him a good home," David
said, apologetic.

"Well, I don't know. We'll think about it."

Early one fall morning a young cowboy friend came
by to visit with David. After seeing Skidboot, he told
David, "You need to cut that cow dog's tail off."

Say what? *You lost your mind, boy? They ain't enough of
y'all put together to cut my tail off!*

Skidboot decided maybe this would be a good time
to go to the barn and find Fred.

"God gave him that tail for a reason. I'm sure not
going to cut off something God wanted him to have,"
David remarked.

Skidboot heard David's remark as he headed for the
barn.

Maybe ol' Too Tall isn't such a bad guy.

"Your dog don't mind much, does he?"

"He minds when I want him to mind," David
replied, more than a little annoyed.

That remark got David to thinking. He hated to admit it, but Skidboot not only wouldn't mind, he did what he wanted, when he wanted. Rather than just trying to ignore him as a pest, it was time he took some responsibility for Skidboot. It was high time Skidboot was taught some manners.

Over the past several months, David had noticed Skidboot would watch people and mimic their actions. On more than one occasion when David was limping, he noticed Skidboot limping. He dismissed it as coincidence. But there were times when Skidboot would watch every move he made, and it was almost spooky.

Fred was half asleep on his pile of feed sacks in the barn. Things were looking up for him. All of Blue Bell's puppies had been adopted and were gone. Skidboot hadn't been quite as aggravating, so life was good.

Skidboot was just about to the barn when a mean-looking pit bull dog stepped into the barn door entrance, blocking him from entering.

Hey, where did you come from?

Grrrr . . . grrrr!

Fred heard the growling and looked up to see Skidboot walking up to the snarling pit bull dog.

Stay back, Shorty ... he'll hurt you. That's one mean dude.

Skidboot stopped in his tracks, first looking at the intruder then at Fred.

Fred got to his feet. The hair on his back stood up as he slowly walked toward Skidboot. He always saw himself as someone who'd rather talk his way out of a bad situation than have any kind of conflict. But this was a *real* bad situation.

Hey, buddy, we don't want any trouble, so why don't you just turn around and walk away?

Grrrr ... grrrr ... was the only response.

Your vocabulary is somewhat limited, isn't it?

For the first time since the bull incident, Skidboot was sensing real danger. He hadn't moved a muscle since Fred told him to stop. He stood staring at the dog's eyes, and it was a scary thing to see.

What should I do?

Just stay where you're at. We'll work this out.

Fred approached within a few feet of the intruder.

My name's Fred, what's yours?

Grrr . . .

Oh, boy, this is not good.

Fred stopped and glanced toward David, who was in a heated discussion with his visitor. Out of the corner of his eye he saw Blue Bell coming out of the tack room.

What's going on?

Stay back, Blue Bell! We've got ourselves a problem.

Blue Bell stopped short of Fred, who was now facing the bull dog.

This is our home, and if you can't behave yourself you'd better leave now.

Grrr . . . grrr . . .

Skidboot, you turn around and go to the house. I mean right now.

Skidboot didn't know what to do. Fred told him to stay still, and Blue Bell told him to leave.

While Skidboot was thinking about what to do, the pit bull leaped at Fred.

Fred had turned to face Blue Bell when he caught a glimpse of the dog attacking. His natural reflex was to avoid him. But he was caught off guard, and before he could move, the pit bull was on him, snarling with massive teeth snapping.

Skidboot froze. He'd never seen a dog that aggressive.

Fred knew he was fighting for his life. He went nose to nose, tooth to tooth with the bigger, muscular dog.

David heard the two dogs fighting and ran toward them, shouting, "Get out of here, dog!"

In just seconds Fred had suffered a gash on his shoulder and front right leg. Overmatched, he gamely continued to fight off the aggressive dog. But it was obvious it was just a matter of time before Fred was hurt bad or even killed.

David leaped into the melee, attempting first to shove the two dogs apart. But the bull dog had a death grip on Fred's neck.

David knew he had to do something, and do it fast. He had heard horror stories about pit bull dogs grabbing other dogs around the neck and not letting go until the dogs died. He also heard if you grabbed the aggressor by the tail, pulling it straight up, the dog would release its grip.

Fred was exhausted and was having trouble breathing as David grabbed the pit bull dog's tail and pulled upward hard as he could.

Fred felt the dog's death grip relax. He attempted to stand and continue the fight, but his legs buckled and he collapsed.

"Get out of here!" David shouted, as he kicked at the retreating bull dog.

The bull dog slinked off behind the barn and disappeared into the trees to wherever he came from.

Skidboot ran to Fred, licking him on the head.

Are you okay?

Fred could only raise his head. He was still gasping for breath.

David carefully lifted Fred up in his arms and carried him to the front porch. He had forgotten about his cowboy friend until he spoke.

"That was one mean dog. Is your dog okay?" he asked, leaning over David's shoulder.

"I don't know. There's blood everywhere. His hair is so thick and long I can't tell where the blood's coming from," David replied, as he attempted to locate the wounds.

Skidboot was stunned. All he could do was watch as David examined Fred's wounds. He had never witnessed such violence in his young life, and somehow, he knew his life would never be the same. He had lost his youthful innocence.

"I've got to trim all that long hair around the

wounds to be able to doctor them. If you'll watch over him I'll get the clippers from the barn," David said. He stood up and hurriedly walked toward the barn.

Blue Bell was standing next to Skidboot, watching David from the porch steps.

Skidboot turned and faced Blue Bell.

Will he be okay?

I don't know. He looks like he's hurt bad.

Why did that dog fight him? Fred didn't do anything to him.

I don't know. Some dogs are just like some humans—just plain mean, I suppose.

Both Skidboot and Blue Bell watched as David carefully trimmed Fred's long hair from around the wounds.

"Well, the good news is I don't think any of his wounds will require stitches, but he's still cut up just the same. His leg is already swelling, and he's sure going to hurt for several days," David commented, relieved at least that Fred would recover.

"Does that dog belong to a neighbor?" the cowboy asked.

"I don't know where he came from. He don't belong to any of my neighbors. I imagine he's a stray. Town people drop 'em off in the country thinking someone will take 'em in. But what usually happens is that they'll get run over or starve to death. That bull dog was probably someone's cute little pet when he was a puppy, but when he grew into an overaggressive adult dog they didn't know what to do with him, and just dumped him."

"Man, that's cruel."

"Happens all the time."

After cleansing and medicating Fred's wounds, David carried him into the house and made him comfortable.

Skidboot and Blue Bell watched as David carried Fred into the house.

Wow, Fred really fought hard. I didn't know what to do. Fred told me to leave him alone, and I did. But then he jumped on Fred for no reason. I was afraid. But Fred wasn't.

Fred is brave. He was just protecting you. I suppose it's just instinctive. Something bred in Border collies.

Wow, protecting me? I didn't think he even liked me.

Remembering Fred's attempts to rid himself and the ranch of Skidboot, Blue Bell wasn't sure how to answer.

Well … er … I suppose he must have cared for you, or he would have just stayed out of it.

Fred was confined to the comforts of home for several days. He was treated like the hero that he was by the whole Hartwig household. Russell was there to feed and pet him, and Barbara fixed special dishes for him. Fred was a happy dog.

Skidboot, on the other hand, missed Fred. But he didn't like Fred getting all of the attention. Several times he was told: "Leave Fred alone . . . he needs his rest." It was beginning to get old.

After a morning of just drifting around the ranch, he decided to pay a visit to the pond. Chasing livestock was not much fun anymore. And he wasn't ready to wander far off from the ranch, especially without Fred. For some reason he didn't fully understand, he didn't take the same pleasure in aggravating David as he did before.

He had forgotten about the ducks that frequent the pond. As he approached, his attitude improved considerably.

There were at least two dozen ducks leisurely swimming in the pond just asking to be chased. He sneaked closer and closer until he got to the edge. Then he leaped into the water.

Ducks went everywhere. Most flew away, but a few just swam out to deeper water.

Not to be outdone, Skidboot swam after them.

You cannot escape Blue Thunder!

But they did. After several attempts, Skidboot got tired of the game and started swimming toward the bank.

He was almost to shore when he felt a sharp pain on his jaw. He shook his head and saw a long, dark object slink away.

Wow, what was that? Whatever it was, it sure did hurt.

By the time he reached the shore, he had a sick feeling.

Must have been a snake. Fred warned me about them. I guess I forgot.

He ran toward the house hard as he could. The pain in his jaw hurt more each time he took a step. By the time he ran up on the porch, his jaw was twice its regular size.

He whined and scratched on the door, but no one came.

Then he saw David and Barbara coming from the barn. He ran past David to Barbara.

Help me! I'm snake bit, I think.

"Oh my goodness, look at his jaw!" Barbara shouted.

David examined Skidboot's jaw and looked up at Barbara. "He's been snake bit."

"Oh no, let's get him to the vet."

David carried Skidboot to the truck, and they raced him to the vet's office.

Be careful, Too Tall, I'm hurt bad. Maybe even worse than Fred.

The vet confirmed that indeed Skidboot had been snake bit. He thought that other than feeling a little bad for a couple of days and having a swollen jaw, he would be just fine.

But for Skidboot, it didn't seem fine. He'd never hurt so much or felt so bad in his young life.

For the next several days, Fred and Skidboot had a contest to see which one could get the most sympathy. But time passed quickly and they both recovered.

Fred returned to the barn and his comfortable feed sacks. Skidboot returned to his corner in the house. For some reason that Skidboot didn't understand, things seemed different. Maybe he was just growing up.

Chapter 6
Life Changes

While David was saddling his bay mare to go check cattle, he kept thinking about Skidboot and how he had changed in the last several weeks. His whole attitude was different. Now he was eager to help, but just didn't know how. He would attempt to help David herd cattle, but mostly he just ended up scattering the herd. That meant extra time spent rounding them back up, and time was something David didn't have a lot of. If Skidboot were trained, he could provide the help David needed.

David had been reading articles on how to train a cow dog and found out that a heeler will only push or drive cattle away from the handler. So, with Skidboot being a heeler, he instinctively drove cattle away from David. That caused a problem when David needed to head cattle and change directions.

David finished saddling the mare. As he mounted, he glanced down at Skidboot. Another big change was

that Skidboot had become his shadow. Everywhere David went, Skidboot was right with him. If he went to work cattle, Skidboot was there. If he went somewhere in the truck, Skidboot leaped up in the truck bed.

"Well, Skidboot, let's go check the cattle. There are a couple of old cows we might have to bring up to the barn. They had a hard time calving last year, so I'd feel better if they were where I could keep an eye on 'em."

Okay, boss, let's do it. Time's a wasting.

David touched the bay with a spur. The mare untracked and eased into a running walk, with Skidboot following a few feet behind.

As he headed toward the pasture, David couldn't help thinking about the way Skidboot looked at him when he spoke. The dog seemed to understand every word he was saying. He would move his head side to side and make barely audible noises in his throat. He seemed to be attempting to answer. David knew that was impossible, of course. Skidboot was just a dog.

David rode into the herd and separated the two old cows, then started driving them toward the holding pens. Skidboot positioned himself behind the cattle.

This is all right, David thought, as he and Skidboot eased along behind the cows.

David stepped down to open a gate when one of the cows, well known for being ornery, made a break back to the main herd.

"Dang," David shouted, hurrying to remount.

Soon as the cow turned and ran, Skidboot ran after her. He was doing what he was bred to do—keep cattle going forward and away from the handler.

"No, Skidboot, whoa! Stop . . . quit! Don't run her," David shouted as he spurred the mare forward in an attempt to head the cow and turn her back.

The faster the cow got, the faster Skidboot chased her until she ran back into the herd.

As David slid to a stop, he looked down at Skidboot.

"Skidboot, this ain't working. We've got to figure out how to train you. We're not getting anywhere like this. I need help, not hindrance."

Skidboot looked up at David, expecting to be praised for a job well done.

Okay, boss, what's next?

After a lot of shouting, arm waving, and a certain amount of threatening language, David finally herded both cows into the holding pens.

That night he told Barbara somehow they had to train Skidboot, and the first thing he had to learn was to whoa. If they could just get him to stop when told to stop, they would at least have a starting point.

A few days later, David was reading an article in a horse magazine. It was about how to train a dog to whoa. He immediately called Skidboot from Russell's room to give it a try.

Skidboot eased into the living room and stood looking up at David.

Okay, boss, what's the deal?

"We're going to teach you how to whoa," David said, looking at Skidboot.

Say what?

Barbara couldn't help smiling. There stood David, telling a dog he was going to teach him something.

David followed the article exactly. He got down on his knees behind Skidboot, surrounding him with his arms. When Skidboot would attempt to walk off, David would tighten his arms, saying: "Whoa!"

After only three or four times, David would tell Skidboot to whoa, and he would stop.

David and Barbara couldn't believe how fast Skidboot responded.

"Can you believe that?" David said, turning to Barbara.

"No, I can't. I thought he was smart, but that's almost unbelievable."

Skidboot had several toys they let him play with when he was in the house, more to keep him out of trouble than anything else. David took one of the toys and tossed it across the room. Skidboot immediately ran for the toy.

"Whoa!" David shouted.

Skidboot stopped in his tracks.

David and Barbara were amazed.

Hearing the commotion, Russell came in to see what was going on.

"Watch this," David said, tossing the toy across the room. Once more Skidboot ran for the toy.

"Whoa!"

Once again, Skidboot stopped and stood motionless, looking at the toy but not approaching it.

"Wow, that's great! When did you teach him that?" Russell asked.

"About two minutes ago," David said, proudly.

Skidboot was still standing and staring.

"Shouldn't he get a reward?" Barbara asked.

"You're right." David moved closer to Skidboot and said, "Get the toy, Skidboot."

Skidboot leaped and grabbed the toy, shaking it so violently he almost fell on the slick floor.

For several days David worked on the two commands: "Whoa" and "Get it." He couldn't believe how fast Skidboot learned.

David decided to give Skidboot a real test. He turned a calf into the arena. Then he told Skidboot to "go get him." As soon as Skidboot was almost behind the calf, he shouted, "Whoa!"

Skidboot slid to a stop.

The next thing he taught him was to back up. David did it the same way he taught Skidboot to whoa, except hc would pull back on him, telling him to back up, then release pressure as soon as he backed. Once again, it took only three or four sessions, and Skidboot would back up on command.

After those early successes, David was convinced that everything he taught Skidboot had to be taught from behind. Whether it be lying down, shaking hands, wait, or whatever, David never faced Skidboot when teaching him a command.

After learning each command, Skidboot would look at David.

Hey, what's the big deal? All you have to do is show me what you want.

One day Barbara met David at the door. She was so excited she could hardly talk.

"Watch this," she said, positioning herself over Skidboot on all fours.

As she and Skidboot eased across the floor she would push against Skidboot's back to the point he was crawling. She would tell him "Crawl, Skidboot," as they moved across the floor.

"Isn't that something?" Barbara said proudly.

"I've been told that once you push a dog down to make him crawl, you'll have to do it every time thereafter," David said.

"I don't think that's right," Barbara countered.

"Well, it won't take long to find out . . ."

Barbara stood up and said, "Crawl, Skidboot."

To both their amazement he crawled across the room until Barbara shouted "Whoa!"

"Well, you sure showed 'em wrong about that one," David commented, still not believing what he had witnessed.

Skidboot continued to learn every command David and Barbara could think up. It was remarkable. He and David became inseparable. Whenever David went to shoe horses or to rope, Skidboot went along and would entertain everyone with his antics.

Feeling a little sorry for himself, Skidboot decided to see what Fred and Blue Bell were doing. It had been several weeks since his last real visit with either of them. While David was shoeing a horse, Skidboot slipped off and went looking for them.

He found Fred fast asleep on the front porch, and the thought crossed his mind about leaping on top of him. But it just didn't seem the same.

He sat down next to Fred and watched him snore away. After a few minutes, Skidboot decided to wake him up.

Arg . . . Sniff-sniff . . .

Fred opened one eye, then shut it.

Hey, Fred, you awake?

No . . . What do you want? Your boss run you off?

Nope. Thought I'd just see what you been up to.

Same o', same o' . . .

Where's Blue Bell?

Keeping track of her is not one of my jobs.

Have you seen her today?

Why don't you go find her and leave me alone?

All of a sudden, it hit Skidboot: He didn't have anything in common with Fred anymore, if he ever did.

Well . . . I'll see you then.

Yeah . . . Later.

Fred went back to his nap while Skidboot searched for Blue Bell.

He found her lying on Fred's feed sacks in the barn.

Hello, Skidboot.

Morning! Is Fred sick or something?

I don't believe so. Why do you ask?

I tried to talk to him, but he wasn't interested.

Well . . . You're grown up now. And Fred is Fred. He helped with your education in his own way, but now you're going down your own path, and it's different from Fred's and mine. It's going to be an exciting life, too. I knew when you were just a puppy you were different from the others. You will be fine . . .

Skidboot didn't understand exactly everything Blue Bell said. But he did know that his life, as he had known it, would never be the same.

Chapter 7
The Making of a Celebrity

David worked with Skidboot every chance he got, but with shoeing and training horses, caring for cattle, and going to rodeos, there wasn't a lot of time to spend training. So, a lot of Skidboot's training and education was accomplished during those activities.

One day at a roping, David was waiting his turn to rope. To kill a little time he was showing some of the cowboys a few of Skidboot's tricks. When he lifted his leg up, Skidboot did the same. Thinking that was part of the act, all the cowboys laughed. Skidboot, being the showman he is, took notice. David did it again, and Skidboot did the same thing. Everything David did, Skidboot would mimic him. David would lay down and roll over. Skidboot would roll over. No commands were given. He would just watch David and do whatever he did. The cowboys were amazed.

Several of them suggested he should take their act on the road.

That got David to thinking . . . Why not?

After that day, every spare minute David could find was spent working with Skidboot. He was an excellent student.

David never liked giving a direct command like "Whoa" or "Back up." He just thought it was not polite. So after every command he would add, "Please." Also, Barbara didn't like "Whoa," so it was changed to "Wait, please."

One summer evening after Skidboot and David had returned from a roping, Skidboot went looking for Fred and Blue Bell. It seemed like it had been a year since the last time he talked with them. Soon as David opened the truck door, Skidboot slipped out and headed toward the barn.

He found Fred lying on the sunny side of the barn, right about where he thought he would be.

Hey, Fred, what's up?

Fred had been taking a nap after eating a big meal but saw Skidboot coming.

Not much. Hadn't seen you around in a while. You and the boss still getting along okay?

Yeah, I suppose. Seems like about all we do anymore is

do those stupid tricks over and over. We don't have fun anymore. It's all work and more work.

Well . . . one has to do what one has to do.

Why didn't you ever do tricks?

I'm a little smarter than some give me credit for. I've got a good life. I eat, sleep, kind of come and go when I want, and nobody bothers me. Russell gives me a pat on the head every once in a while, so life is good.

Sometimes I wish it was like it used to be.

Well . . . nothing stays the same.

Where's Blue Bell?

In the tack room with another bunch of squalling pups.

When did that happen?

The other day.

Skidboot walked to the tack room door and peered inside. There were at least six squirming puppies all trying to nurse at the same time.

Well hello, Skidboot. You haven't been around lately.

Skidboot couldn't take his eyes off the puppies.

Wow, there's sure a bunch of 'em.

Yes, there's seven all total. You have four sisters and three brothers.

Sometimes I wish I was still a puppy. Being an adult sure isn't a lot of fun sometimes.

Becoming an adult brings adult responsibilities. We can't stay puppies. We all grow up—that is, if we're lucky. I see you going with David all the time and you seem to enjoy being with him.

Yeah, it seemed to be more fun before we got into all this trick stuff. Now we hardly ever work cattle, we just do the same old thing all the time. I suppose some of it's fun. I like performing.

Well, life is like that. We can't always do what we want. We all have to do whatever it takes to get along.

I suppose.

He watched the puppies for several minutes until he heard David calling.

Well, got to go. I imagine the boss wants to train me some more. I can't get it across to him that all he has to do is just show me what he wants and I'll do it.

Humans are like that. You behave and take care yourself, and visit me when you can.

I will.

Skidboot slowly walked back to the porch where David was waiting.

"Come on, Skidboot, we've got a few minutes before dinner. I want to show you something I want you to learn," David said, opening the screen door to let Skidboot in.

Big stinking deal . . .

After hours of practice David and Skidboot had their act honed to perfection. Now all they needed was an audience, preferably a paying audience.

Chapter 8
All in a Day's Work

Midsummer was a time to spray cattle for flies, worm the calves, give whatever injections were required to keep them disease free, and check the whole herd's general health. That meant getting up early and staying late until the job was done.

Skidboot knew when he and David left the house before sunup that they were going to work cattle. He couldn't restrain his excitement.

As David was saddling his sorrel gelding, Skidboot kept running from the tack room to the barn entrance in anticipation. He barely acknowledged Blue Bell and her puppies as he bounded in and out of the tack room.

Hi . . . We're going to work cattle. Bye . . . Come on, boss. Let's get on with it. I'm ready to have some fun.

David tied a lariat rope and a piggin' string to his saddle. This was just in case he had to rope and tie down a cow. Roping a cow was the last thing he wanted to do. It's bad for the animal and dangerous for both horse and rider. But sometimes there isn't an alternative.

The plan was to drive the cattle up from the lower pasture to the working pens. Once safely gated in the pens, David and Skidboot could run the cattle into a working chute. Once secure in the chute, David could work on each individual cow or calf without him or the cattle getting hurt.

David opened the gates leading to the pens as they headed for the big pasture. Skidboot kept running ahead of David.

"Hey, Skidboot, slow down! We've got a long day ahead of us."

Skidboot stopped and looked back at David.

What's taking you so long? It's daylight and we've got cattle to herd. Blue Thunder is ready and willing!

They would be herding sixty head of cows, some with calves, and mixed-age yearling calves. There were two herd bulls, a young mixed Angus, and an older mixed Brahma. The Angus was quiet and gentle, but the mixed Brahma could get stirred up if pushed too hard.

"Okay, Skidboot, let's just move 'em all to the holding pens. Then we'll separate and work 'em one at a time."

The herd was scattered. A few older cows with calves were along the river under trees. Most of the weaned yearling calves and the rest of the cows were out in the open. Neither of the bulls was in sight.

David reined his gelding to a stop and began counting the cattle. He was one yearling calf short and didn't see either of the bulls.

"Come on, Skidboot, let's find the missing calf and locate the bulls," David said, as he nudged the sorrel into a trot.

Skidboot trotted along beside David, raring to go.

David rode along the edge of the river bottom for about half a mile before spotting the calf, or at least what was left of him.

He dismounted Ol' Sorrel, dropped the reins, and bent down to investigate the carcass. David determined the calf hadn't been dead that long. Maybe the night before or even earlier that morning.

Varmints had been eating on him, and he was pretty well chewed up. That made it impossible to tell how he died. There were bobcats and coyotes along the river bottom. Also, there were more and more wild dogs around. So it was hard to say what killed the calf. One thing was certain: It cost David about four hundred dollars no matter who or what killed it.

"Well, Skidboot, there goes the profit for about four or five calves," David remarked, and remounted.

Skidboot smelled the carcass, then quickly backed away.

Coyotes . . .

A little uneasy, Skidboot glanced around for any sign of the coyotes. He had some experience with coyotes before, and that was enough for him.

Hey, boss, this one's dead. Let's get out of here before those coyotes come back to finish the job.

David nudged Ol' Sorrel with a spur, heading farther into the bottom.

They hadn't gone far when David reined his horse to a stop. The young Angus bull was lying down next to the river. He had found a nice cool spot in some high grass and was about half asleep.

Skidboot knew he was there before David ever saw him. He was already positioning himself where he could go after the bull as soon as David told him to.

Okay, bull, I'm coming to get you.

Skidboot was motionless, standing no more than five feet away from the young bull.

David attempted to ride his horse closer, but the brush and tree limbs prevented him from getting any closer.

"Get 'em, Skidboot," David called out.

Skidboot went into action.

Get going, Blacky! You belong to Blue Thunder!

Skidboot leaped at the bull and without making a sound nipped the bull on a back leg. The bull immediately rose to his feet and tried to turn and face Skidboot. But Skidboot was already behind him, nipping. The bull kicked backward at Skidboot, but all he kicked at was air. Soon as his foot hit the ground, Skidboot was nipping at him once more.

Hey, you want to try that again?

Seeing he was fighting a lost cause, the bull made a trail through the brush with Skidboot right on his heels.

Come on back . . . you want some more of me?

Skidboot drove the bull back to the herd, staying right behind him until he heard David.
"Skidboot, wait."
Skidboot, pleased with himself, headed for David.

How's that?

"Good boy, Skidboot, good boy."
That left the older Brahma bull unaccounted for. David started riding circles around the herd until he found the Brahma standing in a stand of scrub trees. He had been standing motionless, and if

Skidboot hadn't caught a glimpse of him they would have ridden on by.

Ah-ha! There you are, bully. Don't you know you can't hide from Blue Thunder?

Skidboot stopped, glancing first at the bull then at David.

David reined to a stop, and saw the bull. "Hey, good boy, Skidboot." He circled the trees, and after some shouting the bull walked out and stood facing David.

This bull was a little ornery at times but had never been bad to fight.

David and the bull stared at each other for what seemed like an hour, then David nudged Ol' Sorrel forward. The old bull didn't move. The closer David got, the lower the bull's head got.

David untied his lariat rope from the saddle horn and built a loop. He didn't plan on roping a bull that size. He just wanted something to swing at him to get him moving.

Just as David swung the rope, the bull charged.

"Skidboot, get him!" David shouted as he spurred Ol' Sorrel away from the charging bull.

Skidboot immediately leaped into action. He grabbed the bull by the back leg. The bull kicked hard at his tormenter. Skidboot had already backed away. The bull's attention was diverted for only a second, and he continued to charge David and Ol' Sorrel. Once again, Skidboot leaped and grabbed the bull by a back leg. This time the bull turned to face Skidboot, but he was already gone. He was behind him.

Hey, dummy, I'm back here. Can't you keep up?

Growling as he did, Skidboot nipped again at the retreating bull's back feet.

David watched as Skidboot pestered the old bull until he trotted back to the herd.

"Good boy, Skidboot, good boy!" David shouted as Skidboot walked up and stood facing David. If David didn't know better, he might have thought Skidboot was smiling.

How's that, boss?

After a couple of circles to get the herd together, it didn't take long to drive them to the working pens. David couldn't believe how well Skidboot had performed. It was even more than he had expected.

By evening David had finished vaccinating the last calf. He opened the gates leading to the lower pasture and let the herd find their own way back.

He led Ol' Sorrel back to the barn, unsaddled him, and turned him out into the corral. David put grain in his feed trough while the gelding rolled.

"Well, fella, we did a good day's work today. *You* especially," David said, reaching down to scratch Skidboot behind his ears. "Good boy."

Skidboot was enjoying the praise about as much as the scratching.

Aw, shucks . . . weren't nothing any outstanding cow dog couldn't do!

Chapter 9
A Star Is Born

David was in the calf roping at Mesquite, Texas, and had arrived early to get the rodeo clown's opinion about Skidboot. David and Skidboot had practiced their act to the point David thought they were ready for a professional performance. But what he didn't know was what other people thought. Other than Barbara, Russell, and a few close friends, no one had seen Skidboot perform.

David and the rodeo clown walked out to David's truck, where Skidboot waited patiently.

"Skidboot, come here," David commanded, opening the truck door.

Okay boss, what's up?

"Skidboot, get in your position."

Skidboot moved close to David's leg and sat down.

"Get the toy," David commanded, as he threw a welder's glove a few feet in front of them.

Skidboot started for the toy.

"Wait, please. Tag my hand first."

Okay, okay, make up your mind. Do you or don't you . . .

Skidboot ran back to David and tagged David's right hand with his front right paw, turned and ran to the glove, grabbing it firmly in his teeth.

By now a sizable crowd had gathered, including a rodeo stock contractor.

"Okay, that's enough. Bring it here," David said holding his hand out.

Skidboot eased up to David and placed the glove in his hand.

"Good boy, Skidboot."

David had Skidboot perform a couple more tasks before telling him to get in the truck.

No one could believe what they had seen.

David turned to the rodeo clown. "What do you think?"

"Man, you've got yourself a sure-fire winner."

While David was talking to the clown, the rodeo stock contractor approached.

"I'm going to produce a rodeo at Blue Ridge in a couple of weeks and I'd like to hire you and your dog for a specialty act. You think you could make it?"

"We sure can. Just tell me when and where, we'll be there."

All the details were worked out, and the deal was finalized right there in the parking lot.

The next day, as David was polishing up the performance, he began to have doubts.

Skidboot had never performed in front of a large crowd. Mostly it had been for neighbors or a bunch of cowboys at a roping. What if he got distracted by the crowd? Or, worst of all, what if he got stage fright and ran out of the arena?

By the time David and Skidboot were leaving for their first performance, David was unsure of everything.

"Maybe it'd be best if we just didn't show up. At

least we wouldn't completely embarrass ourselves," David said, looking at Skidboot.

Hey, boss, what are you worried about? All you have to do is be the straight man. I'll handle the crowd.

After getting parked, David located the rodeo announcer. He told David he'd seen dog acts before. It wasn't hard to tell that he wasn't impressed with David or Skidboot.

David wouldn't have a microphone in the arena, so he would have to talk to the announcer and he in turn would address the crowd.

As the rodeo progressed, David thought about all the things that could go wrong. All of a sudden he heard the announcer over the loudspeaker.

"We have a special treat for y'all tonight. We have an unbelievable dog with his cowboy trainer to perform for your pleasure. It's my privilege to introduce David Hartwig and Skidboot."

David and Skidboot were standing in the alleyway entrance when the spotlight hit them.

"Uh-oh, Skidboot. Here we go," David said, as he removed his hat and walked into the arena.

Skidboot trotted beside David as they entered the arena.

Hey, boss, it's showtime . . .

David positioned himself where the announcer could hear him, but where Skidboot would have room to perform his tasks.

"First thing we want to do for you is fetch," David shouted so the announcer could hear him. The announcer still didn't seem the least bit impressed.

"Now, any dog can fetch, so I want Skidboot to do a little something special before I tell him to fetch," David said, and threw the glove several feet in front of him and Skidboot.

Skidboot sat next to David's right leg, not moving a muscle.

"Now, before you fetch your toy, I want you to tag my hand," David instructed, looking down at Skidboot.

Yeah, I understand. We've been doing this for three months. Let's do it . . .

Skidboot stood up, turned to face David, tagged his outstretched hand with his paw, and ran to grab and shake the glove.

Up to that time the crowd was talking and moving around. Then they all stopped and watched with wonder. Even cowboys getting ready for the next event stopped and watched.

"Well, folks, I told you we had a special treat tonight," the announcer said, finally impressed. "What's next, David?"

"Well, I'm goin' to have Skidboot go pick up his toy when I say *three*."

"You just said *three* and he didn't go get his toy," the announcer remarked.

"Well, you see, I haven't told him to go get his toy yet."

"Okay . . . go ahead."

"Skidboot, get in your position, please," David requested.

Skidboot sat next to David's right leg, looking straight ahead.

How's that, boss?

"Skidboot, when I tell you to get your toy, I want you to tag my foot and go pick up the toy. But don't pick it up until I say *three*. You got that?"

Sure, I got it. Let's get on with it . . .

"Wait a minute, David, you just said *three* again. How does he know not to go get the toy?" the announcer asked.

"It's simple. I haven't asked him to yet."

"Okay, I guess."

"Skidboot, tag my foot and go to your toy, but don't get it until I count to *three*."

Skidboot leaped to his feet, tagged David's right foot, and started to run for the glove.

"Wait, Skidboot. I want you to tag my other foot."

Skidboot immediately turned and ran back to David, tagging his left foot.

C'mon, boss, make up your mind . . .

As Skidboot was almost to the glove, David said, "Wait, I've changed my mind. Back up."

Skidboot slid to a stop and then backed up.

"Back up a little more."

Skidboot backed up once again.

Okay, boss, once was funny, twice is getting old . . .

"Skidboot, turn around please."

Skidboot turned completely around and stood motionless.

"I'm sorry, turn the other way please."

Make up your mind! I'm getting dizzy!

Skidboot turned the opposite direction.

The announcer chimed in. "Wait just a minute. I have to ask. You just told Skidboot to turn around. Then you told him to turn the other way. Both commands sounded the same. I was watching you very carefully and you didn't give him a hand signal. How in the world did he know which way to go?"

"Well . . . If you turn one way and then you're

asked to turn the other way, I would expect you'd turn the opposite direction, wouldn't you?"

"Then he must understand the process of elimination," the announcer added, still attempting to understand.

"Well, yeah, sure he does."

"How do you know?"

"Every time I go barefoot in the backyard I find that out."

"Okay ... sorry I asked. Go ahead with your act."

"Skidboot, get in your position."

Skidboot remained motionless throughout the discussion between David and the announcer.

Come on, boss, this is getting old. Get on with the show.

"Okay, Skidboot you can go get your toy, but remember, don't pick it up until I count to *three*."

Skidboot stopped with his muzzle a few inches away from the glove.

"Okay, Skidboot, I'm going to count and when I say *three* get your toy."

"You did it again, you said *three*," the announcer said.

"But I haven't counted yet. He knows what the rules are," David replied.

"Okay, sorry for interrupting. I'll be quiet."

"Okay, Skidboot, one, two ... four ..."

Skidboot stood motionless.

David continued: "Five, six, fifteen, twelve, ten . . . three."

Skidboot grabbed the toy.

The crowd went wild. Even cowboys behind the chutes stopped what they were doing and walked into the arena to watch.

Skidboot brought the glove back to David and placed it in his hand.

The announcer was excited. "David, I'm going to have to say, I thought this was just another trained dog act, but Skidboot is not just another dog. He's amazing."

The crowd stood up clapping, and the cowboys were whistling and shouting their approval.

A standing ovation took David by complete surprise.

"Skidboot, bow for the nice people."

Skidboot lowered his front legs to the ground and then lowered his head to bow.

Thank you very much. It's my pleasure. I live to entertain. If I'm anything I'm humble.

"I can't imagine how he can top that, but what's next?" the announcer asked.

"Well, Skidboot's going to play dead for us."

"Okay."

By now the announcer had no idea what to expect. David had already exceeded his allotted time. But after glancing at the mesmerized crowd he decided to let David take as much time as he wanted.

"Skidboot, play dead."

Oh no, not that old trick. Man, this is embarrassing.

Skidboot lay down.

"Okay, Skidboot, get up," David asked.

Skidboot didn't move.

"Hey, it's time to come alive," David repeated, nudging the motionless Skidboot.

No reaction from Skidboot.

David reached down and pulled Skidboot's back end up by his tail. Skidboot was like rubber. Soon as David released his grip, Skidboot lay motionless.

"I saw this on the television show *Bay Watch* one time, so I'm going to try it on him," David announced as he kneeled next to Skidboot's motionless body. "Skidboot, do you hear me?"

David turned Skidboot's limp muzzle up as if he was going to give him CPR.

"Skidboot, if you can hear me, touch my hand."

Come on, boss. Any mutt can do this one.

Skidboot reached out and touched David's outstretched hand.

"He's still alive, y'all."

"I'm going to revive him," David said as he pushed three times on Skidboot's side.

Then David blew on Skidboot's mouth and pushed three more times on his side. He attempted to pick up the limp Skidboot, but the dog just flopped down.

"I don't understand. It always works on *Bay Watch*," David said, as he put his hat over Skidboot's head.

"Oh my gosh, now what do you do?" the announcer asked.

"I'm going to try cowboy CPR."

"What's cowboy CPR?"

"I'm goin' to threaten him."

"How's threatening him going to do any good? You already gave him CPR with no response. He looks dead to me," the announcer said, really getting into the act.

Come on, boss, get this over with. Lying in this hot, itchy sand is not what I call fun.

"Skidboot, if you don't come alive by the time I count to three, we'll just go ahead and bury you. Okay, here goes. One . . . two . . . three."

At the count of three Skidboot jumped up and ran to find his toy.

Man, I'm glad that's over with.

The crowd went wild.

"I don't know how you can top what y'all have done. I'm afraid to ask what's next."

The rodeo crowd was still on their feet clapping while the announcer was attempting to talk with David.

"We're going to do 'copy me.'"

"Copy me?"

"Yeah, I'll do something and Skidboot will copy me."

"Okay."

David lifted his right leg. Skidboot lifted his front right leg. With his leg still lifted, David shook his foot. Skidboot did the same. Then David lifted his left leg. Skidboot did the same thing.

The crowd responded with loud applause.

David got down on all fours and began to crawl. Skidboot did the same.

Okay, boss, here's a little extra something.

While David was crawling, Skidboot rolled over.

"Wait, just a minute," the announcer said. "I thought this was copy me. Who's doing the copying? You or Skidboot?"

Caught by surprise, David shouted, "We are."

"Well then, why did Skidboot roll over before you did?"

Yeah, answer that one, boss.

"Well, maybe he decided I needed to copy him," David said, as he rolled over.

Soon as David rolled over, Skidboot did the same.

The crowd watched in disbelief, then went wild with applause.

David took his hat off and turned to Skidboot. "Bow for the nice people."

No problem, I aim to please.

Skidboot bowed as David bowed his head.

As Skidboot and David ran from the arena, the crowd continued to applaud.

"David Hartwig and his Amazing Cow Dog, Skidboot, rodeo fans," the announcer shouted. "Maybe

they'll be back later. That is, if you want them to."
That remark caused another round of applause.

Soon as David cleared the arena, he bent down and gently scratched Skidboot behind the ears.

"Skidboot, you did great. It was better than I ever expected."

Skidboot was enjoying the scratching and the praise as well.

All in a day's work of your typical superintelligent and humble cow dog.

David was walking back to his truck when a man hustled up to him.

"Can I ask you a few questions?"

David really wanted a few minutes to unwind, but he stopped and waited for the man to approach.

"I have a grand champion Rhodesian ridgeback. He's been judged grand champion all over the nation."

"Sir, I'm sure you have a wonderful dog, but I really don't know anything about your kind of dog. Matter of fact, I'm not a dog trainer," David responded, a little impatient sounding.

"That's what I wanted to tell you. It shows you don't know anything about training a dog."

Uh-oh, David thought, *I don't like the way this conversation is headed.*

"What do you mean?" David asked.

"It shows you're not a dog man because you break every rule of dog training."

David stared at the man, thinking he wanted out of this conversation. "I'll take that as a compliment."

"You should . . . I meant it as a compliment. There's no way that dog should be able to do the things he does."

"Well, he does. You saw him."

"Yes, I did, but I still don't know how."

"Well, it's pretty simple to me. I just tell him what to do and he does it," David answered, a little puzzled.

"But you don't understand. That would mean he has cognizant reasoning."

David thought that sounded like he had some kind of disease and couldn't help but laugh to himself.

"No, that's impossible. He's been vaccinated for every disease," he replied, smiling as he said it.

That remark caused the man to laugh as well. He realized that whatever training methods David used were going to remain David's secret.

On the way back to the truck, David decided he would use the cognitive reasoning in his shows.

Their last performance of the night was for Skidboot to run the barrels. As the last barrel racer completed her run, David walked into the arena.

"What are you doing out there? Your act is over," the announcer said.

David and the announcer had already worked out the routine after Skidboot's remarkable performance.

"I'm sorry, but I think there's one more barrel racer."

"Okay, get out of the way so we can finish up."

David moved to the fence and waited. Earlier, David had talked a cowboy friend into being with Skidboot while David stood in the arena. Skidboot knew what was next and waited anxiously in the arena alley.

When David shouted to start, Skidboot came tearing out the alley toward the first barrel.

The crowd shouted encouragement as Skidboot flew perfectly around the barrel pattern. He made a barrel run that would be the envy of any barrel racing horse.

When Skidboot finished his run, the announcer called out his time. "He not only ran a flawless pattern, he did it in eighteen seconds flat."

The crowd was still clapping when David and Skidboot came into the arena for one last bow.

On the way home, David turned to Skidboot.

"I have no idea what you're thinking or what you think of me, but you're finally living up to the potential I thought you had all along."

Oh, yeah? That ain't the way I remember it. But I think you're pretty cool, too.

Chapter 10

Ranch Work Never Ends

David and Skidboot had just returned from an extended personal appearance tour. While they enjoyed performing, both were looking forward to returning to the ranch and everyday work. Barbara and Russell had been taking care of feeding the livestock and other day-to-day chores. But with Barbara working full-time away from the ranch, it was difficult to stay caught up.

As David and Skidboot headed for the barn, a neighbor pulled into the driveway.

"I believe one of your cows is in my pasture, David," the neighbor said, getting out of his truck.

"I wouldn't be surprised," David replied, offering his hand.

Uh-oh, I was looking forward to just doing nothing for at least a while.

"What did she look like?" David asked.

"I really haven't got a good look at her. She's pretty well staying back in the brush away from my cows. But she looks like a red-colored cow with a little white on her face."

"Oh boy, yeah, I know which cow it is. She's a heavy springer. I figured she would have calved by now. I've been gone for about two weeks and was just going to check the herd when you came up."

"Well, sorry to bring bad news."

"Oh no, I appreciate you coming by," David said, waving goodbye to his neighbor. "Well, Skidboot, I guess we know what we'll be doing today," David said, as he scratched Skidboot behind the ears.

Yeah, I know. Oh well, what the heck. All in a day's work for a cow dog. Even an exceptionally intelligent, good-looking, celebrity-type cow dog.

After feeding, David hitched up the twenty-foot gooseneck trailer, then pulled up to the barn. He caught Ol' Sorrel and saddled the old gelding. If he got into a storm with that cow, he wanted a horse he could trust.

Skidboot walked around the barn, still expecting to see Fred and Blue Bell. They both had passed away last fall, and he still missed them. He wished now he had spent more time with them. But now, as an adult, he knew nothing stays the same and life goes on.

David loaded Ol' Sorrel into the trailer, grabbed his catch ropes, and shouted for Skidboot.

"Come on, Skidboot. It won't do any good to try to hide. We still have to go get that cow."

Okay, okay, don't hurry me, boss.

David climbed into the truck cab and opened the door for a reluctant Skidboot.

"Maybe it won't be too bad," David remarked. But, knowing the history of this particular cow, it wasn't going to be easy.

After opening his neighbor's gate, David pulled through and shut the gate behind them. His plan was to drive as close as he could to the cow. He would get her out of the brush and rope her, then drag her into the trailer. With Skidboot behind her, David was hoping it would work.

It was a larger pasture, mostly open with scattered mesquite trees except in the river bottom. The area where David's neighbor had seen the wandering cow was covered in fallen trees and head-tall brush.

David drove as close as he could to the bottom before unloading his horse. He tied his catch rope to the saddle horn, tightened the cinch on the gelding, and mounted.

"Okay, Skidboot, let's see if we can find that ol' outlaw," David said, nudging his horse into a running walk.

Lead on, boss, I'm right behind you.

After about an hour of searching, Skidboot's head came up.

"Do you see her, Skidboot?"

Energized by the hunt, Skidboot was ready and willing.

Yeah, boss, there the ol' girl is. She thinks she's hiding, but no beast can hide from Blue Thunder.

David glanced around but still didn't see the cow. He remembered his other encounters with this same cow and none of them were good. She had horns and would fight if pushed. Many times David wished he had dehorned her. The only reason he kept her was that she raised a good calf every year.

Come on, boss, she's standing right over there by that brush pile. How do you ever get anything done without me?

David caught a glimpse of the cow and turned Ol' Sorrel around.

"Okay, Skidboot, here's the plan. You get her out into the open and let's drive her close as we can to the trailer. I'll rope her, and between the two of us we'll drag and prod her into the trailer," David instructed. He untied his catch rope and built a loop.

Sounds like a plan. Let's do it!

As David waited in the open pasture, Skidboot eased behind the cow and waited for David's command.

"Skidboot, get her!"

Skidboot leaped into action. He ran at the reluctant cow, barking and nipping at her back legs and feet until she moved forward. The old outlaw was almost out of the brush when she caught sight of David and his horse. She immediately turned to get back to the safety of the brush.

Oh no, you don't. No cow turns back on Blue Thunder . . .

Skidboot would run at the cow, nipping as she attempted to hook him with her long, sharp horns. By now the cow was slobbering mad and was looking for anything she could take it out on. She gave up trying to hook and kick her blue-colored tormenter and moved out into the open pasture, where she saw David and Ol' Sorrel.

David had been watching as Skidboot drove the cow out of the brush. The first thing he noticed was that she was not springing. That meant she had had her calf. Up until then, he hadn't seen any sign of the calf. While he was thinking about the calf, the cow was closing the distance between them at a rapid pace.

Skidboot was right on her heels when David yelled, "Skidboot, wait!"

Skidboot slid to a stop.

Now what, boss?

David watched as the cow approached, closer and closer. She always had a bad temperament, but now she was red-eyed mad. It looked like David and Ol' Sorrel were her targets.

David took up on the reins and nudged Ol' Sorrel to get ready to react. Then he shouted to Skidboot: "Skidboot, get 'em!"

Skidboot leaped into action, circling and nipping at the cow's heels.

David, seeing an opening, nudged Ol' Sorrel forward and roped the mad cow slick around the horns. Taking a dally around the saddle horn, he backed Ol' Sorrel until he felt the rope tighten around the cow's horns and saw her head come around.

Now David had the full attention of the cow. She quit fighting Skidboot and ran at Ol' Sorrel. David reined the old gelding quickly to the right of the cow and spurred Ol' Sorrel. When the cow hit the end of the rope, Ol' Sorrel, being the good cow horse he was, braced himself for the jerk. Skidboot ran right in behind the cow, keeping her attention while David positioned the horse off to the side of her with his rope tight.

"Skidboot, wait."

Now what, boss?

Skidboot stopped and backed away from the cow.

"Let's just let her settle for a minute," David said, sitting quietly but alert on Ol' Sorrel.

The cow was still mad, but she was also out of breath. David rode up enough to just let her have enough slack where the rope wasn't choking her, but where he could tighten it up if needed.

They stood for several minutes, each watching the other. It was a cow-versus-cowboy standoff.

David glanced toward the truck. It was a good several hundred yards away. He wished it was closer. The cow weighed at least nine hundred pounds, and David didn't look forward to attempting to drag her that far. Ol' Sorrel was a big, stout horse weighing around eleven hundred pounds, but he was also not as young as he used to be.

As David was pondering his alternatives, the cow made up her mind. She decided to make a run for it.

David spurred Ol' Sorrel into a run after the cow. He kept just enough tension on the rope so his horse couldn't step over the slack.

The cow was heading toward the trailer, so David let her run. Just before they reached the trailer, she made a right turn, heading away from the trailer. David spurred Ol' Sorrel forward, then veered to his left. Taking the slack out the rope, he jerked the old cow's head up. Before she could plant her feet, he pulled her to the back of the trailer.

David had left the trailer gate open when they left. He stood facing the winded cow. Both Ol' Sorrel and the cow were blowing hard.

After letting the horse get his breath and while the cow was calm, David eased the tail of his catch rope in between the two top rails of the trailer and quickly positioned Ol' Sorrel facing away from the trailer and dallied the rope. Turning to face the waiting Skidboot, David said, "Skidboot, get 'em!"

Skidboot immediately nipped at the cow's heels

until she lunged forward. As she did, David nudged Ol' Sorrel forward, taking out the slack and moving the cow closer to the trailer opening.

Then, all at once, the cow leaped into the trailer in an attempt to get away from Skidboot. David reached over and shut the divider gate.

Skidboot backed away, satisfied the cow was secure.

What did I tell you, cow? Nothing or nobody escapes Blue Thunder. You belong to me . . .

David stepped down from Ol' Sorrel. After tying him to the trailer and loosening both front and back girts, he said, "Good job, fella." Reaching down, David scratched Skidboot behind the ears. "Good job, Skidboot."

Good job? That's the best you can come up with? How about outstanding job?

After reaching through the trailer bars and removing his rope from the cow, David wondered what happened to the calf the cow had been carrying.

"Skidboot, there's a calf out there somewhere. I suppose we need to look for it," David said, as he tightened Ol' Sorrel up again.

Oh boy, work is never done.

They searched for at least an hour before Skidboot smelled the calf carcass.

Wow, here it is! Or, at least what's left of it.

David saw Skidboot stop and go into a brush pile.

"Find him?" David asked as he dismounted and led Ol' Sorrel to Skidboot.

David stood looking at the calf carcass. It had been dead for several days. That was why the old cow didn't want to leave and fought so hard. She was still protecting her calf, even though it was dead.

"Well, Skidboot, there goes any profit from that ol' cow for a year. I feed her for almost a year for nothing," David said, stepping up on Ol' Sorrel.

David loaded the horse in the trailer and they headed home.

"Well, Skidboot, at least we got the cow. Maybe she'll have a good calf next year."

Skidboot was already asleep in the seat next to David.

Chapter 11

The Tonight Show

David, Barbara, and Skidboot had a few days off and were getting some well-deserved rest when David received a call from the producer of Jay Leno's *Tonight Show.* Jay Leno had seen David and Skidboot on PAX-TV and wanted them on his show.

David was completely taken by surprise. He and Skidboot had been featured on several national televised programs, but David considered the *Tonight Show* to be one of the best. He immediately confirmed that indeed he and Skidboot would be there on the requested date.

"You'll never believe who just called," David said to Barbara, hanging up the phone.

"I can't imagine."

"A producer for the Jay Leno *Tonight Show,*" David said, with a grin.

"Really?"

"Yep, next Wednesday. They said they'll send us our airline tickets and hotel reservations right away."

"When would we leave?"

"I believe they said on Tuesday. I'm not sure. It took me by surprise."

Barbara went to her desk, checking the events calendar. "You have a performance at Sherman, Texas, at twelve noon for the Kiwanis Club on Tuesday."

"Okay, we'll just have to work around it. They're supposed to call in the morning confirming everything."

"That's pretty short notice. We'll have to get everything ready right away."

"Hear that, Skidboot? We're going to be on national television!"

Skidboot looked up from his corner of the couch.

Whatever . . .

The next morning the show producer called with their agenda. They had arranged for Barbara, David, and Skidboot to leave Dallas/Fort Worth (DFW) airport at 4:00 P.M. the next Tuesday. Jay Leno wanted Skidboot to have his own seat. They would stay at the Burbank Hilton Hotel. A limo would pick them up at the airport and would be available to them for their stay in California.

The next few days were filled with preparing for the trip and doing ranch chores. Russell would have to take care of everything while they were gone.

Barbara's sister lived in California and made plans to attend the show with them.

Tuesday morning started early. While Barbara finished packing, David fed and did the few chores that needed doing. He pulled their old 1976 motor home to the driveway and finished loading all the luggage. By 10:30 A.M. they were on their way to Sherman.

The performance went as planned, and they were on their way toward DFW by 1:00 P.M.

David decided he'd better fill up with gas at McKinney, Texas, about halfway between Sherman and DFW. Everything was still on schedule until he attempted to start the motor home.

"Uh-oh," David said, as the starter ground to a halt. "We're in trouble. This thing is dead as a doornail."

"Now what?" Barbara asked.

"Go call a taxi while I see if I can get this thing going," David said. He ran out and opened the hood.

Skidboot looked from David to Barbara.

This is not good. Not good at all . . .

Barbara went inside the service station to call a cab as David pulled and banged on everything under the hood. Giving up, he began unloading luggage.

"They said it would be at least an hour before they can get here," Barbara shouted.

"That's too late," David shouted back.

David jumped in the motor home and hit the starter one last time. The starter growled and groaned. Then, to David's surprise, it started.

"Quick! Load everything back up," David shouted, leaping out the door and slinging luggage back inside. If Skidboot hadn't jumped to the side, he would have been crushed by a suitcase.

Hey, watch where you're throwing that stuff!

Skidboot moved back away from the door and out of range.

"Hurry, Barbara," David said, leaping into the driver's seat.

Barbara was attempting to get seated when David roared off.

"Slow down! You're going to kill us all, the way you're driving," Barbara said, attempting to find something stable to hold on to.

After several close calls and a lot of fist shaking at David over his driving, they pulled into the parking lot forty-five minutes before flight time. Close, but workable.

David dropped off Barbara, Skidboot, and their luggage and parked the motor home. He then ran to the bus stop, out of breath, just as the bus pulled up.

"I made it," David gasped, "two bad hips and all."

David began loading luggage when the bus driver saw Skidboot.

"I'm sorry, sir, but I can't let the dog on the bus unless he's in an animal carrier."

"Mister, this dog has more manners than most people. He's been all over the country. I'll guarantee he'll behave himself," David pleaded.

Skidboot stood looking up at the driver.

Hey, bud, what's your problem? I'm a ticketed passenger, you know.

"And he has a reserved seat," David added.

A woman with a dog stepped off the bus and walked toward the parking lot.

"That dog wasn't in a handler," David said, pointing to them.

"She has a card saying the dog is for handicap assistance," the bus driver says.

"Well, I have bad hips, and this dog gets things for me. I don't know how I'd make it without him," David tried.

Oh man, we're really grasping at straws now. But I do have to admit that he can't do without me.

By now Barbara was wishing she were somewhere else.

"I'm sorry, sir, but without a carrier or handicapped documentation I can't let you on the bus."

The bus drove away with Barbara, David, Skidboot, and luggage on the curb.

"Now what?" Barbara asked.

"Find a phone," David replied, looking around. He ran into the bus waiting area and called airport staff. After what seemed like hours of explaining the situation, they finally sent a shuttle to pick them up.

By the time the shuttle arrived, it was almost time for their flight to leave. David ran back to the phone and called the show staff. They assured him they would have them on the next flight out in one hour.

When they arrived at the ticket line, it looked two hours long. They only had forty-five minutes.

As they waited patiently, an airline official approached.

"I'm sorry, sir, but a summer embargo prevents dogs from flying. It's just too hot in the cargo area."

"You don't understand . . . he's a ticketed passenger," David said.

Skidboot was sitting quietly at David's feet, looking very unconcerned.

Man . . . sure are a bunch of people. Where are they all going?

"The dog has a ticket?" the woman asked.

"Yeah, here it is," David said, holding the ticket out for her to see.

She walked away and came back in a minute with a computer printout.

"Is this Skidboot?" she asked.

"Yes, it is."

"Well, okay, he's flying on celebrity status. Please follow me."

Skidboot trotted along behind David and Barbara with his head held high.

Well, it's about time someone realized I am a celebrity and showed the proper respect!

After being escorted through security, they were boarded and seated before general boarding.

"Well, we made it," David sighed.

"I had my doubts," Barbara replied, making sure she was still in one piece.

They had three seats in the middle of the aircraft. Skidboot sat in the middle seat, with Barbara and David on either side in an aisle seat.

As passengers boarded, they did double-takes when they saw Skidboot sitting up straight in his chair, watching everything and everybody. Several people remarked that they didn't think a dog could travel in coach. Another said he was probably a dog that assisted a disabled person. One of the passengers had seen Skidboot at the State Fair of Texas and began telling anyone who would listen who Skidboot was.

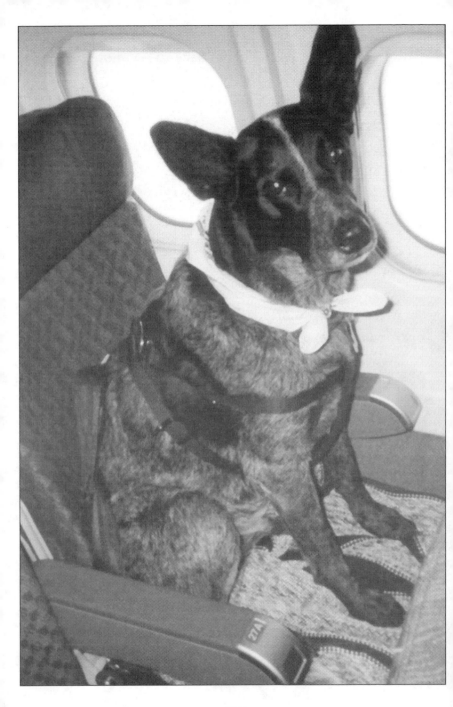

After takeoff, passengers would file by to see him and talk briefly with David and Barbara.

Hey, I'm the celebrity! Talk to me!

When dinner was served, Barbara fed Skidboot with a fork as he sat up straight and ate with better manners than most people. Everyone was amazed, and the flight attendants asked for "pawographs."

When the plane landed, the pilots wanted pictures of Skidboot in the cockpit with their pilot hats on him.

Skidboot took all the attention in stride. It was all part of being a celebrity. If a person didn't know better, it appeared Skidboot was smiling. He glanced at the cluster of instruments, then looked up at David.

I could fly this thing, you know. This is something I could really get into.

After they got their luggage, a limo driver met them and hustled them off to the hotel.

The hotel staff was expecting them. They were quickly ushered to their suite.

"Man, look at this!" David said, glancing around. "We're sure not in Texas."

"I'm worn out," Barbara said, sitting down in the first chair she came to.

"Look, they have a basket of fruit and dog treats for Skidboot," David said, holding up the basket.

Skidboot walked over to the basket and looked at it.

Don't see anything in there I like. Where's the beef?

After a well-deserved night's sleep and breakfast, they called the limo service to pick them up. The limo picked them up and drove to the NBC studio. The show producer met them at the studio door and escorted them to their dressing room. The dressing room had Skidboot's name with a big star on it.

Okay . . . these people know how to treat a star!

The dressing room had a couch, several chairs, and a table with a big basket full of food—both human and dog selections. The segment producer then came in to give them the agenda for the day.

"I need to find out what you and Skidboot plan to

do," she said, "then we have to write a script for you and Jay to follow."

Uh-oh, David thought, *this is not going to be easy.*

Okay, boss, don't panic. I'll get you through it.

David told the producer they would do the fetch, count, and copy-me routines. He could tell she didn't understand.

The longer they waited, the more nervous David got. Barbara knew everything would go just fine. He and Skidboot had gone through this before and everything went fine.

Just about the time David was going to break and run, the producer escorted David and Skidboot to the studio for rehearsal. Barbara found a seat so she could watch.

Someone stood in for Jay Leno while David and Skidboot went through their routines. The stage and camera crews couldn't believe what they were seeing. It took longer than normal to rehearse because they got so engrossed in watching Skidboot.

"I've never seen anything remotely like that dog," the segment producer said, approaching David. "Do you think we could get him to get out of the limo and walk up to the studio door by himself? That would make a terrific lead-in for the show."

"Sure, he'll do anything you ask him to," David replied.

It took a few minutes to get the limo in position, and to add a final touch they laid a red carpet from the limo to the studio door.

David walked with Skidboot to the limo. He opened the door, and Skidboot jumped in the back seat.

"Okay, Skidboot, when I call you I want you to slowly walk to me at the studio door."

David walked back to the studio door. When the limo driver opened the door, David called to Skidboot.

"Okay, Skidboot, slowly walk to me."

Hey, who's the star here? I know how to walk.

Skidboot looked as if he was swaggering as he walked. The film crew was laughing. David wasn't sure what to say.

"If I hadn't seen it, I wouldn't have believed it," the producer said.

After the rehearsal, David, Barbara, and Skidboot were escorted back to the dressing room. David asked if there was a place outside they could go to unwind. The producer told them they could go to the Johnny Carson Park on the studio grounds if they liked.

The park had trees and grass, offering a place for Skidboot to run off some energy. David stretched out on the grass, and Barbara found a bench under a shade tree.

All too soon it was time to go back to the dressing room to meet with Jay Leno before taping the show. David kept telling himself these were just nice common folks, no reason to be nervous.

Jay walked in with a big smile and his hand outstretched. "Hello, I'm Jay Leno," he said, shaking hands with David and then Barbara.

"I'm David Hartwig, and this is my wife Barbara," David responded.

"Glad to meet you, Barbara," he said, shaking hands with Barbara.

"Nice to meet you."

"And *this* is Skidboot," Jay said, looking at the star.

"Yep, that's Skidboot," David replied.

"Can I touch him? I know a lot of dog trainers don't like anyone touching their dogs," Jay asked.

"Mr. Leno, I'm not a dog trainer, and I sure don't mind you petting Skidboot."

Hey, am I not here? I don't need someone making decisions for me. I'm an adult. You can pet me if you want.

Jay got down on one knee and rubbed Skidboot along his back.

I'll give you an hour to stop that.

"Skidboot, I saw you on PAX-TV and I couldn't believe what you did. You're really something."

125

Thank you very much. It's nice to be appreciated.

"I'm not sure what I'm supposed to do," David said.

"They're going to bring us a script in a minute. But it's just something to kinda keep us on track. We're just going out there and have fun and let Skidboot do his thing."

The producer brought in the script, and Jay and David talked through it.

David felt better after meeting Jay and going over the script. Now he had a good idea about what they were going to do.

After another twenty minutes, Jay had to leave. "I'll see you and Skidboot in a few minutes," he said.

It wasn't long before the stage manager escorted David and Skidboot to a position by the studio curtain. Another staff member escorted Barbara to her seat, where her sister and brother-in-law were already seated.

The longer they waited the more anxious David got.

Hey, boss, everything will be okay! Just follow my lead.

David heard Jay introduce them, and thankfully his feet responded. He walked onto the stage with Skidboot beside him.

"I know you've met a lot of dogs in your life, ladies and gentlemen, but this is the greatest dog I've ever seen. You're not going to believe this dog. Skidboot's his name, and David Hartwig is his owner. They have a great trick they call 'sneak up on it' and they're going to do it for us. Please welcome David Hartwig and Skidboot from Quinlan, Texas."

"Thank you very much," David said, reaching for Jay's hand.

"Sit right down here," Jay said, shaking hands with David.

They both sat down, Jay behind his desk and David at his side.

"That's a good-looking dog."

"Thank you."

Why are you thanking him? It was me *he said was good looking.*

"Skidboot, get in your place," David requested.

Skidboot moved around to David's right leg and sat down.

Give me a break. How many times have we done this? I could do it in my sleep.

"Where is Quinlan, Texas?"

"It's east of Dallas about forty miles."

"What do you do down there? Sell insurance, stocks and bonds?"

"I'm a horse shoer."

"Good for you," Jay said, touching David on the

arm. "A horse shoer . . . okay. What kind of a dog is Skidboot?"

"He's half blue heeler and we didn't know his daddy so we just say the other half is a gift from God."

"That's a good way to put it . . . Where did you get him?"

"On the job. I was out shoeing horses on Christmas Eve and hadn't got a present for my wife yet."

"Wait a minute, wait a minute . . . A typical guy. It's Christmas Eve and you haven't got a present for your wife. Checked the trash, nothing there," Jay said, smiling.

"I had one more customer with four horses to shoe. He doesn't raise dogs, but he had this litter of heeler pups in his barn from a stray female. I didn't need another dog, but I did need a Christmas present. So I went ahead and had to take one home."

"Christmas Eve . . . stray dog . . ."

"It's the truth."

"Okay, I believe you," Jay said, laughing. "This is your wife's present."

"Yeah, I was driving home and something made me go back and switch. I had just picked up the prettiest, fattest one. I didn't check to even see if he could hear or whatever. So, I went back to Butch's place and told him I wanted to change dogs. There was one off by himself looking around, and I told Butch I'd just take that dog."

"Let's bring him over here," Jay said, moving from

behind the desk. "What's the first thing you want to show us?"

"We'll start with tag and fetch. Come here, Skidboot," David said. "Get in your place."

Here we go again.

"Now, I want you to fetch, but you've got to follow the rules. If you want the toy you got to tag my hand," David said, tossing the toy a few feet in front of them. "Skidboot, tag my hand," David said, holding his hand out.

Okay, boss.

Skidboot reached out with his front right paw and tagged David's hand, then ran to the toy. Just as he grabbed it, David shouted.

"Skidboot, put it down. I've changed my mind. I'm not a very good dog trainer. I can't make up my mind," David said, turning to face Jay. "Skidboot, I want you to tag Jay's foot."

Okay, okay . . . just make up your mind.

Skidboot ran back to Jay and tagged his foot and ran for the toy. The audience went wild.

"Skidboot, give me the toy please," David requested.

You're a confused man, boss.

"Everybody says I don't give him treats, and I didn't want to train my dog to treats. Can you see me horseback and have to get off and tell the guys 'Wait a minute, I've got to give him a cookie?'"

I don't know about that. Sounds like a pretty good idea to me.

"No, no, no . . . you don't want to do that," Jay replied. David handed a biscuit to Skidboot to hold at the very edge of his lips.

You know I don't like these things. One day I'm going to fool you and not eat it.

"I'm going to give him a treat, but I want to read the ingredients off the box," David said. "There's fat."
"Oh, that's no good," Jay said.
"It's got protein. It's got fiber. On the bottom it's got what he was looking for . . . vitamins."

Okay, here's my cue.

Skidboot grabbed the biscuit in his teeth and swallowed it.

Man, that's some bad stuff!

The audience laughed and clapped.

"That's a good one. How about 'sneak up on it'?" Jay asked.

"Okay, Skidboot, get in your place."

This is getting old, boss. If I know anything, I know my place.

"I'm going to throw his toy right over here," David said, as he tossed the toy a few feet in front of them. "Skidboot, sneak up on your toy."

With his head held low, Skidboot slowly sneaked toward the toy.

"Wait, Skidboot."

Skidboot stopped, motionless.

"Back up."

Skidboot backed up.

"Back up once more."

Skidboot backed again.

"Okay, go ahead."

Skidboot moved very slowly toward the toy.

"Nope, that's too close. Back up."

Skidboot slowly backed up.

"Turn around."

Skidboot turned around.

"I mean the other way."

C'mon, make up your mind!

"Okay, get close ... A little closer ... That's too close. Back up."

Skidboot backed up.

"Bow, Skidboot."

Skidboot bowed.

This is getting embarrassing ...

"Okay, Skidboot, get your hand up."

Skidboot raised his left front paw.

"No, I meant your right hand."

Skidboot raised his front right paw.

"Okay, get a little closer."

Skidboot moved closer to the toy.

"A little closer."

Skidboot's muzzle was no more than three inches from the toy, and he was frozen.

"Now, here's the rules. When I count to *three* you can get the toy but not before I say *three*. But don't forget, when I say *three,* get it. I'm going to trick you, so you better listen carefully. One ... two ... four ... seven ... nine ... eleven ... fifteen ... three ..."

Skidboot grabbed the toy, giving it a good shaking.

Take this, you troublemaker.

The audience went wild.

"Ladies and gentlemen, David Hartwig and

Skidboot," Jay said, pointing to David and Skidboot as they left the stage.

After the show was taped, David and Skidboot met with Jay and other guests for pictures. Everyone wanted a picture taken with Skidboot. Even the film crew got involved.

After a long flight and a long trip home from the airport, the weary travelers arrived at the ranch. As David and Barbara were unloading the luggage, Skidboot headed for the barn. He walked throughout the barn and tack room, sniffing. Fred and Blue Bell had been gone for quite a while, but their smell still lingered. He saw the pile of feed sacks that Fred used to sleep on. It was like something was pulling him toward them. He slowly walked over and lay down.

Fred, old friend, I've been on a big adventure. But not like the ones you and I used to have . . .

His eyes got heavier and heavier, and closed.

Still Working Like a Dog

David continues to actively shoe and train horses for the public and stays busy with the endless daily tasks of ranch work. His days start early and end late. But, to quote David, "It's not work if you enjoy it."

Skidboot remains his constant companion and eager assistant. He is there to help David with every cow that's branded or doctored. As a team they entertain appreciative audiences across the nation with David's cowboy humor and Skidboot's uncanny intelligence and showmanship.

In spring of 2003 Skidboot was in the spotlight of national television, appearing twice on the *Oprah Winfrey Show* and becoming a finalist on Animal Planet's program, *Pet Star*. The duo is regularly featured at the State Fair of Texas. A video starring Skidboot and David titled *Skidboot: Making Friends* was released in late 2002.

For the latest Skidboot news, performance schedules, and video ordering information, visit skidboot.com on the Internet.

About the Author

RON WESTMORELAND, a lifetime horseman and rodeo cowboy, was born and raised in Fort Worth, Texas. Ron is a member of the Western Writers of America and is the author of several books, including *I'm Not Dead Yet* and *Remember That Ol' Horse*. He teaches cre-ative writing at Collin County Community College and still enters roping competitions in "old-timer rodeos." Ron has been married to his childhood sweetheart, Betty Ann, for fifty years, and they have three children, eight grandchildren, and four great-grandchildren. He lives in Caddo Mills, Texas.

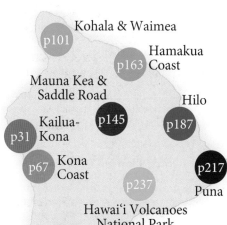

Kohala & Waimea
p101
Hamakua
p163 Coast
Mauna Kea &
Saddle Road
Hilo
Kailua-
Kona   p145   p187
p31
Kona
p67 Coast
p217
p237   Puna
Hawai'i Volcanoes
National Park
p271 Ka'u

This Is Hawai'i the Big Island

We doubt it's possible to get 'island fever' on Hawai'i. The aptly named Big Island is fantastically diverse, with miles of highways and – better yet – *byways* to explore. From age-old fishing villages to modern mega resorts, from snow-capped peaks to sandy beaches, you'll experience tropical splendor backed by an epic history. Hawai'i is twice as big as the other Hawaiian Islands combined, and its dramatic terrain will surprise you and take you to extremes.

At 800,000 years old, Hawai'i is a baby in geologic terms. It's here you'll find the Hawaiian Islands' highest and largest volcanic mountains – and the world's most active volcano, spewing molten lava since 1983. Circumnavigate the island and watch stark lava desert morph into rolling pastureland and misty valleys, weathered by rain, waves and time.

Ancient history looms large on Hawai'i, a place of powerful mana (spiritual essence). The first Polynesians landed at Ka Lae, where the windswept coast remains pristine and undeveloped, and Kamehameha the Great was born in North Kohala. Hula and *oli* (chant) are powerful forms of living history, and the Big Island has spawned legendary hula masters and the celebrated Merrie Monarch Festival.

Plantation days are long past, but not the colorful legacy. The waves of immigrants who labored in the cane fields added their languages, foods and cultures to the mix. Today, there's no ethnic majority and common bonds are intangible: the pidgin vernacular, easygoing manner and deep love of the *'aina* (land).

Hawai'i is surprisingly untouristy. And thanks to its sheer size, there's lots of legroom. While the South Kohala Gold Coast caters to travelers en masse, most island towns are rural and cater to residents. Even the capital seat, Hilo, is a former plantation town that's still slow-paced and populated by *kama'aina* (born-and-raised Hawaiians). Wherever you go, there's a sense of freedom and frontier. The Big Island is a guaranteed *big* experience.

> " Wherever you go, there's a sense of freedom and frontier "

Waipi'o Valley (p172)

Hawai'i the Big Island

PACIFIC OCEAN

155°30'W
156°W
20°N
19°30'N
19°N
156°W
155°30'W

Upolu Point
Mo'okini Luakini Heiau
Hawi
Kapa'au
Makapala

Kapa'a Beach Park
Mahukona
Mahukona Beach Park
Lapakahi State Historical Park
Kahua

NORTH KOHALA
Pololu Valley
Kohala Mountains
Kukuihaele
Hamakua Coast

Kawaihae
Spencer Beach Park
Hapuna Beach State Recreation Area
Puako

Kohala (5480ft)
Waipi'o Valley

SOUTH KOHALA
Waimea (Kamuela)
Mana
Kalopa State Recreation Area

Honoka'a
Pa'auilo

Kohala Coast
Kiholo Bay
Kiholo
Ka'upulehu

Waikoloa Village
Waimea-Kohala Airport
Saddle Road Junction

Keanakolu Rd
Keanakalu

Queen Ka'ahumanu Hwy

Mauna Kea (13,796ft)

Kekaha Kai State Park
Wawaloli (OTEC) Beach
Kalaoa

Kona International Airport at Keahole

NORTH KONA
Onizuka Visitor Information Station
Saddle Rd

Kaloko-Honokohau National Historical Park
Honokohau Harbor
Kailua-Kona
Kailua Bay
Palani Junction
Mt Hualalai (8271ft)

Holualoa

Keauhou

Mauna Loa Observatory Rd
Northeast Rift Zone

Haleki Bypass Rd
Kona Coast

Kealakekua
Captain Cook
Kealakekua Bay State Historical Park
Kealakekua Bay

Honaunau
Pu'uhonua o Honaunau National Historical Park

Ho'okena

Mauna Loa (13,677ft)

Hawai'i Volcanoes National Park

SOUTH KONA
Hawaii Belt Rd (Mamalahoa Hwy)

Mauna Loa Rd

Miloli'i
Miloli'i Beach Park

Kauna Point

Manuka State Wayside Park
Road to the Sea

KA'U
Wai'ohinu
Na'alehu

Pahala
Ka'u Desert
Southwest Rift Zone

Punalu'u
Punalu'u Beach Park
Honuapo
Whittington Beach Park

Pohue Bay

South Point (Ka Lae)
Green Sands Beach

PACIFIC OCEAN

Hawaii Belt Rd
Southwest Rift Zone
South Point Rd

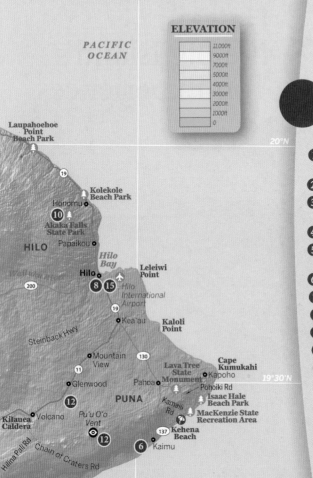

ELEVATION

11,000ft
9000ft
7000ft
5000ft
4000ft
3000ft
2000ft
1000ft
0

0 — 40 km
0 — 20 miles

155°W

PACIFIC OCEAN

20°N

Laupahoehoe Point Beach Park

19

Kolekole Beach Park

Honomu

10

Akaka Falls State Park

Papaikou

HILO

Hilo Bay

Hilo

Leleiwi Point

8 15

Hilo International Airport

200

19

Kea'au

Kaloli Point

Steinback Hwy

Mountain View

130

Cape Kumukahi

Lava Tree State Monument

Kapoho

19°30'N

11

Glenwood

Pahoa

Pohoiki Rd

PUNA

Isaac Hale Beach Park

12

Kamaili Rd

MacKenzie State Recreation Area

Pu'u O'o Vent

Kilauea Caldera

Volcano

12

137

Kehena Beach

6

Kaimu

Hilina Pali Rd

Chain of Craters Rd

19°N

155°W

15 Hawai'i the Big Island's Top Experiences

Hawai'i Volcanoes National Park

The eerie glow of a lava lake, secluded palm-fringed beaches, ancient petroglyphs pecked into hardened lava, and miles of hiking trails through smoking craters, rainforest and desert – what's not to love about Hawai'i's number one site? For a singular experience, try and snag one of the 12 coveted spots on the weekly Secret Lava Tube Tour (p255). This national park (p240) is one of the island's top spots to experience Hawaiian culture including hula on the crater rim, annual festivals and lecture series.

Mauna Kea Star Party

It is breathless *and* breathtaking in the rarefied air of Mauna Kea (p145), Hawai'i's most sacred spot. Once the sun goes down, the stars come out and with them telescopes for your viewing pleasure (p152). The world's clearest stargazing is here – what you see through those telescopes, you won't soon forget. For a real trophy experience, head here for the sun- and moonrise.

Snorkeling in Kealakekua Bay

It's all true – from the teeming, colorful fish in knee-deep water to spinner dolphins lazily circling your kayak or catamaran. Tourist brochures hype this as the best snorkeling (p78) in the state and, in this case, you can believe it. Even new rules regulating kayak use can't tarnish the luster of this must-see spot (p80). If kayaking doesn't float your boat, hike down to this historically significant and naturally brilliant bay. Hardcore environmentalists might consider other less-trafficked bays – this one is almost too popular for its own good.

HAWAI'I THE BIG ISLAND'S TOP 15 EXPERIENCES

Waipi'o Valley

Legends begin where the road ends overlooking this magical valley (p172). You can linger at the scenic viewpoint but the waterfalls, wild horses and wilder black-sand beach beckon. Choose from hiking, horseback or even mule-drawn wagon to get you here. The very experienced can kayak in – when conditions are just right. The most spectacular views are from the grueling switchbacks of the Muliwai Trail (p176) – head up, up and up some more for the money shot.

The Best...
Hikes

KILAUEA IKI TRAIL
Hawai'i Volcanoes National Park's top day hike. p251

MULIWAI TRAIL
Ends at a glorious, waterfall-flanked valley and beach. p176

NAPAU CRATER TRAIL
This hike gets you as close as possible to the active Pu'u 'O'o Vent. p256

HILINA PALI TRAIL
Sweeping views over lava fields and the coast are the highlights of this back-country hike. p256

POLOLU VALLEY TRAIL
Your knees will quake and your spirits will soar with the awesome views on this short, steep hike. p133

The Best...
Beaches

Pu'uhonua o Honaunau National Historical Park

⑤

Dotted with ancient temples watched over by menacing idols, a visit to this national park (p84), known as the Place of Refuge, makes a memorable introduction to traditional Hawaiian culture. In fact, there's no better place to gain an understanding of the kapu (taboo) system that governed ancient Hawaii. Look for *honu* (sea turtles) bobbing in the bay, foreshadowing underwater wonders at the nearby snorkeling haven of Two-Step (p86).

GREG ELMS / LONELY PLANET IMAGES ©

HOLGER LEUE / LONELY PLANET IMAGES ©

6 Lava Chasing

If you're lucky (lava is fickle, don't you know?) you may get the chance to see live lava flowing over and under the land in or around Hawai'i Volcanoes National Park (p250) and ending with a magnificent plunge into the sea, sending a steam plume over a mile skyward as hot lava is mixed with roiling surf. Feel the heat on a walking or boat tour (p223) out of Puna. Kids love the latter – even willful teens will ooh and aah audibly during the volcano's full sensory show.

Hapuna Beach

Rock up to this half-mile powdery white-sand beach, rent an umbrella and a boogie board, and one of Hawaii's most iconic beaches is your playground (p118). Surfboard, lounge chair or water wings – this beach has something for the whole family. While the basic A-frame cabins here are not for the finicky, the island's best beach is your front yard – pretty hallucinatory.

Merrie Monarch Festival

What you saw at the luau? That's to hula what Velveeta is to cheese. If you really want to see how a hula *halau* (school) invokes the gods and legends through chant and dance, time your visit for this statewide hula competition (p202). Book early; people fly in from all over the globe for this one. Unless you're a hardcore hula fan, you are likely to enjoy the inaugural invitational more than the structured head-to-head competitions of subsequent days.

Manta Ray Night Dive

Diving at night is a thrill in itself (p39), but once you turn on your light and attract a corps de ballet of Pacific manta rays, with wing spans of 10ft or more and tails like javelins, your life becomes segmented: before diving with mantas and after. Snorkeling (p44) with them can be even better because you're closer, but it's so popular don't be surprised when you get head-whacked by someone's fins. Bring your own dive light and swim onto center stage with these graceful animals.

⑨

The Best...
For Kids

SNORKELING OR WHALE-WATCHING CRUISE
Moorish idols or humpback whales – thrilling wildlife watching awaits. p335

ZIPLINING
Hands on the cable, heart in your throat on this exhilerating ride. p339

KIKAUA BEACH
This protected cove is perfect for little ones learning to swim or snorkel. p97

KAPOHO TIDE POOLS
Even teens gush about these liquid oases filled with fish. p230

KULA KAI CAVERNS
Huge caverns with geological wonders make a fun and educational family outing. p284

© STEPHEN FRINK COLLECTION / ALAMY

Akaka Falls State Park

This 420ft waterfall (p182), crashing through the rainforest choked with fragrant ginger and giant philodendrons, is no less spectacular for its easy access. Drive up, stroll a half mile through what feels like Hollywood Hawaii and there you are. Like all waterfalls on this part of the coast, the Akaka Falls are most impressive during seasonal rains when they spill violently over the verdant cliffs. Don't miss poking around the little town of Honomu (p182) once you're done ogling these towering falls.

The Best...
Adventures

LAVA BOAT TOUR
Feel the heat on this seafaring adventure to the lava sea entry. p223

NIGHT SNORKEL WITH MANTAS
Float above as these creatures turn graceful somersaults in the dark depths. p43

HIKING TO POHUE BAY
A hot hike across old lava seems like a colossal waste of time – until you reach this secret beach. p284

LEARN TO SURF
Experience the magical alchemy of water, waves and determination required by the 'sport of kings.' p333

LEE FOSTER / LONELY PLANET IMAGES ©

Hiking into Pololu Valley

Waipi'o Valley or Pololu Valley (p132)? It's a tough call as to which emerald valley threaded with waterfalls and blessed with a black-sand beach is more beautiful, but little Pololu retains a tranquility lost to Waipi'o since the invention of the monster truck. It takes a 10-minute downhill hike to get here, but it's the only way in. A visit can easily be combined with a stroll through diminutive Kapa'au (p130), followed by lunch in lovely Hawi (p127). This northern thumb of land is old Hawai'i at its most evocative.

Underground Explorations

In Hawai'i, what you see on the surface is never the whole story. Hardly. Beneath all the forest and flows lie elaborate systems of caves, caverns and lava tubes, multiplying by miles your exploration possibilities. The world's longest lava tube, Kazumura Cave (p224), the world's second-longest, Kula Kai Caverns (p284), and a 'secret' lava tube, Pua Po'o (p255), are among the many options. Exploring these underground formations make a great rainy day activity.

Helicopter Tour

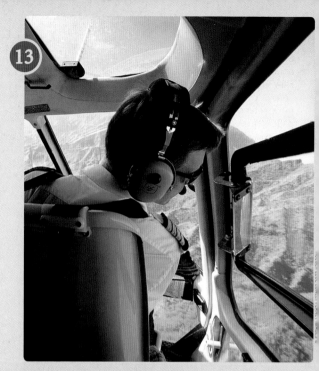

The superlatives flow like lava when people start describing their Big Island helicopter experience (p336). Hovering over the Pu'u O'o Vent, buzzing into Waimanu Valley and zipping alongside verdant valley walls scattered with waterfalls is truly unforgettable. Tours are weather dependent and environmentally debatable. The best time for these flyovers are on clear early mornings, preferably at the end of your trip so you can grasp what you're seeing.

Snorkeling with Sea Turtles

If there was one thing we could be doing from this list right now, it would be getting in the water with these docile creatures. It's a thrill, no matter how many times you do it. Try Punalu'u (p275), Kahalu'u Beach Park (p56) and Kikaua Beach (p97). It might be tempting to treat these animals as you would a house pet, but rules of responsible travel still apply – even underwater.

Stand Up Paddling

SUP! This is what we're talking about: getting out with the dolphins and turtles while getting away from the crowds. How? Just stand up and start paddling. It's easy and a helluva lot of fun. Wildlife watching is particularly thrilling from a stand up paddling board (p333), and stand up paddle surfing makes a bad-ass Big Island memory. When you're ready for something new, rent a board next to the Kailua Pier in Kailua-Kona or in Hilo and hit it!

The Best...
Scenic Drives

KOHALA MOUNTAIN ROAD
Green pastures, black lava and white-sand beaches below a trio of mountains. p127

RED ROAD
Tree tunnels, hot ponds and hippies. p229

PEPE'EKEO 4-MILE SCENIC DRIVE
This jungle ramble crosses rivers and moss-covered bridges. p184

CHAIN OF CRATERS ROAD
This road links volcanic craters like gems on a necklace. p247

WOOD VALLEY ROAD
An enchanted landscape leads to a colorful Buddhist temple. p274

QUINCY DEIN / PHOTOLIBRARY

15

Hawai'i the Big Island's Top Itineraries

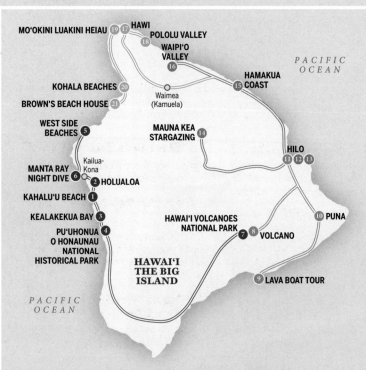

MO'OKINI LUAKINI HEIAU ⑲ ⑰ **HAWI**

POLOLU VALLEY

⑱

WAIPI'O VALLEY

⑯

PACIFIC OCEAN

HAMAKUA COAST ⑮

KOHALA BEACHES ⑳

Waimea (Kamuela)

BROWN'S BEACH HOUSE ㉑

WEST SIDE BEACHES ⑤

MAUNA KEA STARGAZING ⑭

HILO ⑪ ⑫ ⑬

Kailua-Kona

MANTA RAY NIGHT DIVE ⑥ ② **HOLUALOA**

KAHALU'U BEACH ①

KEALAKEKUA BAY ③

PU'UHONUA O HONAUNAU NATIONAL HISTORICAL PARK ④

HAWAI'I VOLCANOES NATIONAL PARK ⑦ ⑧ **VOLCANO**

⑩ **PUNA**

HAWAI'I THE BIG ISLAND

⑨ **LAVA BOAT TOUR**

PACIFIC OCEAN

● **Kailua-Kona to Hawai'i Volcanoes National Park** 4 days

● **Volcano to Hilo** 6 days

● **Hilo to Waipi'o Valley** 8 days

● **Hawi to South Kohala** 10 days

Kailua-Kona to Hawai'i Volcanoes National Park

4 DAYS

Hawai'i Volcanoes National Park (p237)

MARK NEWMAN / LONELY PLANET IMAGES ©

❶ Kahalu'u Beach (p56)

This roadside hot spot teeming with wildlife is great for **snorkeling** or taking a **surfing** or **stand up paddling lesson**.

❷ Holualoa (p62)

In the afternoon, head to Holualoa to browse **fine-art galleries**, sample **Kona coffee** and catch a spectacular sunset.

❸ Kealakekua Bay (p77)

On day two, book a morning **snorkeling cruise** or paddle a **kayak** to the underwater wonders near the **Captain Cook Monument**.

❹ Pu'uhonua o Honaunau National Historical Park (p84)

Take an easy **coastal hike** at the Place of Refuge, where history and nature combine seamlessly.

❺ West Side Beaches (p95)

On morning three, lounge on one of West Hawai'i's famous white-sand beaches.

❻ Manta Ray Night Dive (p39)

Don't miss night diving (or snorkeling) with the giant manta rays near **Kailua-Kona** – it's rated one of the world's top dives.

❼ Hawai'i Volcanoes National Park (p237)

Set out early on your fourth day to visit the world's most **active volcano** (2½ hours from Kailua-Kona) where the popular **Kilauea Iki Trail** and **lava lake** viewing await.

⊙ THIS LEG: 160 MILES

Volcano to Hilo

6 DAYS

Rainbow Falls (p196)

SEAN CAFFREY / LONELY PLANET IMAGES ©

8 Volcano (p264)

On the morning of your fifth day, browse or buy original works – photos, ceramics, blown glass – from the artists who created them at one of myriad **art galleries** dotting moody and romantic Volcano. More active than arty? Try the **Mauna Ulu trail** or the **Kipukapuaulu (Bird Park) hike**.

9 Lava Boat Tour (p223)

The 4:30am start will be worth it when you behold lava gushing into the sea in the predawn darkness. Late risers can opt for a less dramatic daytime or twilight tour. The motion of the ocean makes some horribly queasy – you've been warned!

10 Puna (p220)

Puna is nonconformist and beguiling. Spend your remaining time exploring this region's wonders including **hot ponds**, a new **black-sand beach** and phenomenal snorkeling in lava **tide pools**. At night, head to the **lava viewing area**.

11 Hilo (p190)

Pour yourself into the car after checking out the lava and head a few miles to Hilo to bed down. With its scenic bay, retro downtown and lush greenery, Hawai'i's capital is a real charmer. Stroll downtown to the **East Hawai'i Cultural Center**, stopping for a **homemade ice cream**. For a quick nature fix, head to **Rainbow Falls**, **Richardson Ocean Park** or **Honoli'i Beach Park**.

⬤ THIS LEG: 61 MILES

8 DAYS

Liliʻuokalani Park (p191)

GREG ELMS / LONELY PLANET IMAGES ©

12 ʻImiloa Astronomy Center Of Hawaiʻi (p194)

On day seven, head to this fascinating museum to learn how ancient seafaring, modern astronomy and the Big Islands' volcanic origins converge. If Mauna Kea is on your bucket list, get a mini-education here first. Alternatively, golfers can snag an early tee time at **Hilo Municipal Golf Course**.

13 Liliʻuokalani Park (p191)

Join gaggles of locals (and kids galore) playing at this bayside gem boasting Japanese gardens, pagodas and bamboo groves. Picnic fixings are available at the slow food **Kinoʻole Farmers Market**. Hikers might opt for the 7-mile **Puʻu Oʻo Trail** instead.

14 Mauna Kea Stargazing (p152)

Get up here in time for sunset – the island's top spot for it – and then stick around for free **stargazing**. Taking a highly recommended **summit tour** will maximize the experience.

15 Hamakua Coast (p166)

Begin day eight meandering through storybook rainforest along **Pepeʻekeo 4-Mile Scenic Drive**, before stopping at **Akaka Falls State Park** or taking a local **farm tour**.

16 Waipiʻo Valley (p172)

No matter how you experience this valley – with a guide, on horseback or by wagon tour – it will be memorable. Go solo to explore the **waterfalls** and **black-sand beach** at your leisure. On your way to Waipiʻo Valley, stop in laid-back **Honokaʻa**.

➤ THIS LEG: 91 MILES

Hawi to South Kohala

10 DAYS

Marine life, Puako (p116)

CASEY MAHANEY / LONELY PLANET IMAGES ©

17 **Hawi** (p127)

On day nine, take scenic **Kohala Mountain Rd** to Hawi, a spiffy village and foodie magnet. Try **Sushi Rock**, **Bamboo** or **Luke's Place** for a memorable meal.

18 **Pololu Valley** (p132)

Pololu Valley is smaller and more contemplative than its sister valley Waipi'o – maybe because it sees less traffic. Stop here for some eye candy at the **lookout** or pack a picnic and hike down to the **black-sand beach**.

19 **Mo'okini Luakini Heiau** (p125)

Unless you spent a lot of time swooning over Pololu Valley's rugged beauty, you'll have time to visit this site, one of Hawaii's most sacred. Just near here is **Kamehameha the Great's birthplace**.

20 **Kohala Beaches** (p119)

Spend your last day (we know, we know) kicking back at some of South Kohala beaches – the Big Island's best. Tranquil **Mauna Kea Beach** is an all-time favorite, although many argue **Hapuna** is better. Snorkelers shouldn't miss **Puako**; travelers with very little ones will like **Kikaua Beach** further south.

21 **Brown's Beach House** (p115)

'A gourmet meal can be eaten but once' goes the saying, so make your last one on the Big Island worth it. Splash out at this oceanfront restaurant, the jewel in the **Fairmont Orchid's** dining crown.

○ THIS LEG: 65 MILES

Get Inspired

 Books

○ **Ancient Hawaiʻi** (1998) Renowned artist Herb Kawainui Kane depicts traditional life in vivid detail.

○ **Saturday Night at the Pahala Theatre** (1993) Lois-Ann Yamanaka's bracing stories reveal another side of 1970s Hilo.

○ **Hawaii Big Island Moms & Pops Before Wal-Marts & K-Marts I–III** (2006–10) Wayne Subica shares the good ol' days of family-run shops over three parts.

 Films

○ **Keepers of the Flame** (1988) Eddie and Myrna Kamae (www. hawaiianlegacy.com) profile three legendary Hawaiian women, Mary Kawena Pukui, Iolani Luahine and Edith Kanakaʻole.

♫ **Music**

○ **Four Strings: The Fire Within** (2009) Ukulele prodigy Brittni Paiva's latest collection shows her range.

○ **Kekuhi** (1998) *Kumu hula* (hula teacher) Kekuhi Kanahele's first release epitomizes the power of Hawaiian chant.

○ **Four Hands Sweet & Hot** (1999) Master musicians Cyril Pahinui (slack key guitar) and Bob Brozman (slide guitar) showcase Hawaii's two iconic instruments.

🔊 **Websites**

○ **Mountain Apple Company on YouTube** (www.youtube.com/user/ mountainapplecompany) Watch Israel Kamakawiwoʻole to understand what it means to be Hawaiian.

○ **Toward Living Pono on YouTube** (www. youtube.com/user/ towardlivingpono) Snippets on poi, aloha and the Hawaiian language from iconic Big Islanders.

○ **KonaWeb** (www. konaweb.com) Despite the name, the whole island is covered on this website, with handy links.

○ **HawaiiHistory.org** (www.hawaiihistory. org) Succinct timeline of historical events in Hawaii.

Short on time?

This list will give you an instant insight into the island.

Read *Big Island Journey* (2009) Sophia Schweitzer and Bennett Hymer share Hawaiʻi's rich history with 400-plus vintage photos.

Watch *The Punaluʻu Experience* (2008) Danny Miller's documentary explains why Kaʻu's pristine, black-sand beach is sacred.

Listen *ʻOhai ʻUla* (2010) Kainani Kahaunaele is a gifted composer of *haku mele* (Hawaiian songs).

Log on *Hawaiian Lava Daily* (www.hawaiianlavadaily. blogspot.com) Stunning photos of Kilauea volcano's red-hot lava action.

Hawai'i the Big Island Month by Month

Top Events

 Merrie Monarch Festival April

🍷 **Kona Brewers Festival** March

🎸 **Ironman Triathlon World Championship** October

❋ **Big Island Hawaiian Music Festival** July

🍷 **Kona Coffee Cultural Festival** November

January

❋ **Na Mea Hawai'i Hula Kahiko Series**
Gather at the rim of Kilauea Crater (p260) to witness ancient-style hula and chanting (held five times a year; always on a Saturday).

February

❋ **Waimea Cherry Blossom Heritage Festival**
Celebrate the Japanese tradition of *hanami* (cherry-blossom viewing) on the first Saturday of the month with craft fairs, food booths, live music and other cultural doings.

🎸 **Waimea Ukulele & Slack Key Guitar Institute Concert**
Aspiring musicians can study with Hawaii's foremost musicians at these workshops (p138); concerts and *kanikapila* (jam sessions) open to the public. Held in early February.

March

🍷 **Kona Brewers Festival**
This beer fest (p46) held the second Saturday of the month just keeps getting bigger. Sip handcrafted brews from Hawaii, California, and elsewhere accompanied by good food and live music.

April

❋ **Merrie Monarch Festival**
Hilo's premier shindig is this week-long festival (p202) featuring an intense hula competition among the state's finest hula *halau* (schools). Advance planning necessary.

(left) Kona coffee
PHOTOGRAPHER: ANN CECIL / LONELY PLANET IMAGES ©

May

 May Day Lei Day Festival

This month-long festival (p200) kicks off at Kalakaua Park in Hilo and continues with live music and hula at Hilo's beautiful Palace Theater. Plenty of masterful lei displayed.

June

 North Kohala Kamehameha Day Celebration

Join the celebratory crowds at King Kamehameha's birthplace (p131). Starts with a parade from Hawi to Kapa'au and continues with an all-day hula-, food- and crafts-fest. Similar events are held on Mokuola (Coconut Island) in Hilo.

July

 Kilauea Cultural Festival

For over 30 years, this day-long festival held in early July has drawn crowds to celebrate Hawaiian culture: there's lei and basket-making demonstrations, hula, massage and even nose flute jams.

Big Island Hawaiian Music Festival

A must for Hawaiian-music fans, this two-day concert in Hilo (p200) features virtuoso performances in ukulele, steel guitar, slack key guitar and falsetto singing.

August

 Hawaiian International Billfish Tournament

World-famous fishing competition (p46) held in late July or early August in Kailua-Kona. Watch the weighing of the catch at Kailua Pier.

September

 Aloha Festivals

This statewide Hawaiian cultural celebration (www.alohafestivals.com) runs from late August to early October. It kicks off with the Hawaiian royal procession at Halema'uma'u Crater.

October

 Ironman Triathlon World Championship

Witness human glory and grit when this legendary race comes to Kailua-Kona on the third Saturday of the month.

November

 Kona Coffee Cultural Festival

Celebrate Kona coffee with 10 days of tastings, farm tours and cupping competition to determine the finest crop from estates throughout the island's 'coffee belt' (p46).

December

Mochi Pounding Festival

Join the local community for an all-day party with Japanese *mochi* (sticky-rice cake) pounding, a New Year's tradition in these parts, plus live music.

Holualoa Village's Music & Light Festival

Head upcountry from Kona for the annual lighting of the Christmas tree in this village that is part artists colony, part coffee town (www.hulaalohahawaii.com).

Need to Know

Language
English
Hawaiian

ATMs
Available in all major towns.

Credit Cards
Visa and MasterCard accepted only at larger businesses.

Cell Phones
US phone coverage is good except in remote locations. Asian and European phones work only if they are quad-band.

Wi-Fi
Available at most accommodations; top-end hotels typically charge daily fees.

Internet Access
Internet terminals are scarce; bring your own computer if internet access is essential.

Directions
Makai means 'toward the ocean'; *mauka* means 'toward the mountain.' Refer to highways by common name, not by number.

Tipping
Expected at sit-down restaurants; 15% to 20% of the bill is appropriate.

When to Go

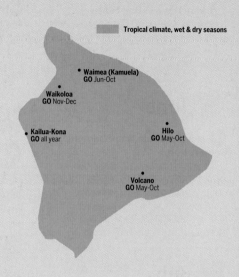

Tropical climate, wet & dry seasons

Waimea (Kamuela) GO Jun–Oct

Waikoloa GO Nov–Dec

Kailua-Kona GO all year

Hilo GO May–Oct

Volcano GO May–Oct

High Season
(Dec–Mar, July & Aug)
- Rates skyrocket at major resorts and hotels
- Winter months bring rain; whale watching is best in February and March
- July and August are also popular with families and students

Shoulder
(Apr–Jun)
- Hilo is booked solid around Easter (Merrie Monarch Festival)
- Rainfall tapers in summer and fall
- Ocean surf is generally calmer

Low Season
(Sep–Nov)
- More vacancies and lower rates for accommodations
- Receive personalized attention at attractions
- Less traffic on highways and roads

Advance Planning

- **Three months before** Decide which region's climate and attractions best match your interests. Search for internet deals on flights, cars and accommodations.

- **One month before** Reserve a spot on popular tours, such as snorkeling, ziplining and Mauna Kea summit. Break in your hiking shoes if brand new.

- **One week before** Confirm your reservations. Check weather forecasts to ensure you pack the right gear.

Your Daily Budget

Budget Less than $150
- Economy hotel or B&B: $60–80
- Eat farmers market produce and takeout meals
- Go swimming and hiking for free

Midrange $150–300
- Midrange hotel or B&B: $125–175
- Eat lunch and dinner at affordable midrange restaurants
- Choose two or three 'must do' guided tours

Top End More than $300
- Major resort in South Kohala or Kona: from $250
- Dinner mains at destination restaurants: $30–50
- Splurge on spa, golf and other resort activities

Exchange Rates

Australia	A$1	$1.03
Canada	C$1	$1.01
Europe (Euro)	€1	$1.41
Japan	¥100	$1.21
New Zealand	NZ$1	$0.76
UK	£1	$1.60

For current exchange rates see www.xe.com.

What to Bring
- **Driver's license** Needed to rent a car.
- **Hands-free device** Using a handheld cell phone while driving is illegal.
- **Hiking shoes** Broken in and sturdy enough for lava-rock terrain.
- **Long sleeves & pants** Light fabric to protect against sunburn and mosquito bites.
- **UV-protection sunglasses** For ocean glare and highway driving.
- **Identification cards** Student, automobile association and AARP cards can be used for discounts.
- **Snorkeling gear** Bring your own if you'll be snorkeling often, or if you're picky about fit and quality.

Arriving on Hawai'i the Big Island

Kona International Airport at Keahole
Car Rental companies located at airport
Bus Limited runs from airport; 50¢ to $1
Taxi $35 to Kailua-Kona; $50 to Waikoloa

Hilo International Airport
Car Rental companies located at airport
Bus Limited runs from airport; 50¢ to $1
Taxi $15 to downtown Hilo

Getting Around
- **Car** Well-maintained highway circumnavigates island. Towns and streets clearly signposted. Free parking widely available.
- **Bus** County bus goes to major towns; limited runs, especially on weekends.
- **Bike** Decent roads for touring. Sun and rain can be brutal.

Accommodations
- **B&Bs & inns** Ranges from budget to luxury; generally reliable; often more spacious and loaded with amenities than comparable hotels.
- **Hotels & resorts** Prevalent in South Kohala and Kona; wide range of prices; top-end resorts offer the best beaches and pools.
- **Condos** Concentrated in Kailua-Kona; ideal for independent travelers who prefer apartment amenities such as full kitchen.

Be Forewarned
- **Rain & floods** In winter expect heavy rainfall everywhere except in Kona and South Kohala.
- **Mosquitoes** Rainforest regions teem with mosquitoes; wear adequate clothing and repellent.
- **Coqui frogs** Nightly mating calls can disrupt sleep; inquire with accommodations if you're sensitive to noise.

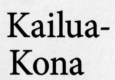

Kailua-Kona

Talk about multiple personalities! Kailua-Kona is first and foremost a quintessential tourist town, with a relentless lineup of coastal condos, souvenir shops and sunburnt pleasure-seekers trolling for a meal or a drink. Further upland, it's old-time Kona in Holualoa, an art mecca in the cool, misty coffee belt.

All the while, the natural beauty of Kailua Bay recalls its original role as an idyllic retreat for Hawaiian royalty. For visitors, Kailua-Kona is a sunny delight and a hub for ocean sports. For locals who like to gripe, it's a sprawling suburb, with pricey subdivisions blanketing the slopes of Mt Hualalai and nightmare rush-hour traffic. (But that doesn't keep them from joining scrums at Costco, Walmart and other big box giants.) Others love the roadside snorkeling with turtles, the annual Ironman action and taking sunset cocktails. It's either for you or it's not. Stop by to find out.

Kailua-Kona Itineraries

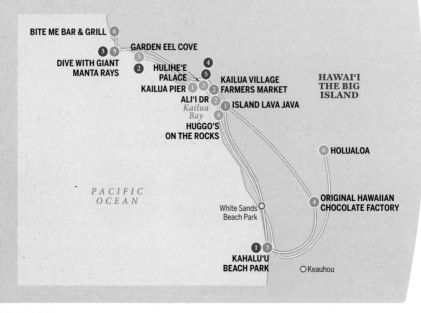

Two Days

1 **Kailua Pier** (p39) Dive into coastal culture with whatever floats your boat – stand up paddling, outrigger canoeing or kayak fishing. Gear and lessons are available right here.

2 **Ali'i Drive** (p49) Stroll along this lively street where you can sample mildly sedative kava (and seriously good *kalua* pig) at **Kanaka Kava** or indulge your sweet tooth with the best locally made ice cream.

3 **Hulihe'e Palace** (p35) Escape the crowds with a visit to this oceanfront landmark, once a royal retreat, now a museum, where artifacts such as King Kamehameha's personal war spears offer a fascinating glimpse into ancient Hawaiian culture.

4 **Huggo's on the Rocks** (p52) Nothing epitomizes Kailua-Kona like catching a legendary sunset with your toes in the sand

and a cocktail in hand. Experience this at Huggo's on the Rocks or head to the upstairs lanai of **Humpy's Big Island Alehouse** for a pint or three.

5 **Garden Eel Cove** (p34) Roll out of bed early and check the weather. Nice and calm? Head to the cove for a morning snorkel. Looking choppy? Join the locals bodyboarding at **White Sands Beach Park**.

6 **Holualoa** (p62) In the afternoon cool off by heading upland to this historic coffee community where farm tours and an art gallery crawl await.

THIS LEG: 22 MILES

32

Four Days

① Island Lava Java (p54) People watching is a hoot at this cafe, with locals zipping along Ali'i Dr on their mopeds and tourists trying to choose from the myriad places to eat. Make a beeline for the outdoor patio to watch it all unfold.

② Kailua Village Farmers Market (p51) Packed with everything from exotic fruits to jewelry and kitsch, the market makes a good post-feast browse.

③ Kahalu'u Beach Park (p56) Snorkel in this pleasantly calm and shallow bay where you're guaranteed to see tropical fish and green sea turtles.

④ Original Hawaiian Chocolate Factory (p59) Candy for breakfast? Huzzah! Kids of all ages will enjoy kicking off the morning with a unique factory tour of the country's only bean to bar chocolate outfit. For even more heavenly delights, follow up your tour with a stop at the **Kailua Candy Company**.

⑤ Dive with Giant Manta Rays (p39) The best nightlife is found underwater cavorting with manta rays. Whether you dive or snorkel with these mesmerizing creatures, they'll play a major part in one of your greatest Big Island memories. And on any given night, **Ocean Wings Hawaii** will probably capture it on video so you can relive the thrill back home.

⑥ Bite Me Bar & Grill (p92) Swap stories and emotions over a glass of wine and tasty fresh fish tacos after your dive.

⇨ **THIS LEG: 20 MILES**

Kailua-Kona Highlights

① Best Beach: Kahalu'u Beach Park (p56) Easy access and abundant sea turtles make this a favorite for locals and tourists alike.

② Best Snorkeling: Garden Eel Cove (p34) Aka Manta Heaven. Enough said.

③ Best Activity: Manta Ray Night Dive or Snorkel (p39) Fiercely popular with good reason; book early.

④ Best Tour: Body Glove Historical Sunset Dinner Cruise (p43) Gorgeous coastal views accompanied by engaging historical narrative, followed by dinner and dancing.

⑤ Best Hawaiian Cultural Experience: Hulihe'e Palace Concerts (p35) Pack a picnic and a blanket for the monthly concert on the seaside lawn.

Kahalu'u Beach Park (p56)
ANN CECIL / LONELY PLANET IMAGES ©

Discover Kailua-Kona

History

For all its tourist-trap vibe, Kailua-Kona holds a significant place in Hawaiian history. Kamehameha the Great lived his last years here, worshipping at Ahu'ena Heiau, his own temple. Soon after his death in 1819, his son Liholiho broke an important kapu (taboo) by dining with women. He suffered no godly wrath, so when the first missionaries sailed into Kailua Bay in 1820 they easily converted the Hawaiians to Christianity.

In the 19th century, the town was a leisure retreat for Hawaiian royalty. Hulihe'e Palace was a favorite getaway for King David Kalakaua, a talented patron of the arts, including hula, music and literature.

Since the 1970s Kailua-Kona has been the Big Island's economic powerhouse, fueled by tourism, retail and real estate.

 Beaches

Kailua-Kona might *act* like a beach town, but its three beaches are not among the Kona Coast's showstoppers. The only swimmable in-town beach is Kamakahonu Beach, a teeny-tiny beach between Kailua Pier and Ahu'ena Heiau, where you can rent all kinds of beach gear and the waters are calm and safe for children.

Ahu'ena Heiau (p38)
JOHN ELK III / LONELY PLANET IMAGES ©

OLD KONA AIRPORT STATE RECREATION AREA Beach
Forget swimming at this sandy but rock-strewn beach. The spacious 217-acre grounds are, however, ideal for picnicking, exploring tide pools and experiencing a locals' beach. There's also a pristine, sandy-bottomed pool for your *keiki* (kids) near the southern entrance gate. At low tide, tiny sea urchins, crabs and bits of coral resemble mini lava rock–aquariums. The old Kona airport was once located here, hence the unfortunate but apt name.

To get here, take Kuakini Hwy 1 mile west from central Kailua-Kona.

From the north end of Old Kona Airport, a short walk leads to **Garden Eel Cove**, a fertile spot for scuba divers and confident snorkelers. Also known as Manta Heaven, this is one of the favored destinations of nighttime tours to see these majestic animals. When the surf's up, local surfers catch an offshore break at Shark Rocks.

Recreation area facilities include restrooms, showers, covered picnic tables, a popular running track and ample parking.

To the south of Old Kona Airport, the **Kailua Park Complex** (☏327-3553; ⏲6:30am-7:30pm Mon-Fri, 8:30am-5:30pm Sat & Sun) offers a pool, gym, kiddy playground, tennis courts, and soccer, football and baseball fields. To get to the complex, take Kuakini Hwy to its end, 1 mile northwest of downtown.

WHITE SANDS BEACH PARK   Beach

Located south of Kailua-Kona along Ali'i Dr, this popular beach is nicknamed Magic Sands or Disappearing Sands; the sand can wash offshore literally overnight during high surf (when the entire park may be closed), exposing dangerous rocks and coral. When the surf settles, however, the sand magically returns. Also known as La'aloa Beach, this compact, roadside beach is always lively and a hot spot for bodyboarding, surfing or just watching the action. Facilities include restrooms, showers, picnic tables and a volleyball court; a lifeguard is on duty here.

 Sights

Ali'i Dr might bombard you with surf shops and ABC Stores, but amid the tourist kitsch are a handful of historic buildings and landmarks. The farmers markets are also worth a look and there are many toothsome eateries. To escape the hordes, pull up a shoreline rock at Hale Halawai Park.

HULIHE'E PALACE   Historical Building

(☏329-1877; www.daughtersofhawaii.org; 75-5718 Ali'i Dr; adult/senior/child under 18 $6/4/1; ⏲10am-3pm Wed-Sat) Imagine the life of Hawaiian royalty in this palace, a simple island manor constructed in 1838 by Hawaii's second governor, John Adams Kuakini, as his private residence. It was originally built with lava rock, but in 1885 King Kalakaua preferred a more polished style after his travels abroad and plastered over it.

After Prince Kuhio inherited the palace from his uncle, King Kalakaua, he auctioned off the furnishings and artifacts to raise money. Fortunately, his wife and other female royalty meticulously numbered each piece and recorded the name of the bidder. Eventually the Daughters of Hawai'i (www.daughtersofhawaii.org), a group founded in 1903 by seven daughters of missionaries, tracked down the owners and persuaded many to return the pieces for public display. In 1973 Hulihe'e Palace was placed on the National Register of Historic Sites.

The two-story palace contains Western antiques collected on royal jaunts to Europe, Hawaiian artifacts and housewares, and a number of Kamehameha the Great's personal war spears.

Navigating Kailua-Kona

You'll notice that locals have multiple names for beaches, breaks and even highways and towns. So it goes with Kailua-Kona – aka Kailua, Kona and Kona town.

Navigating around town can be tricky at first because of this name game: the main highway through town, Queen Ka'ahumana (Hwy 19), confusingly becomes Kuakini Hwy (Hwy 11) at the intersection with Palani Rd, then connects with the historic Kuakini Hwy toward the ocean. In other words, there are two Kuakini Hwys for a stretch.

Kailua-Kona

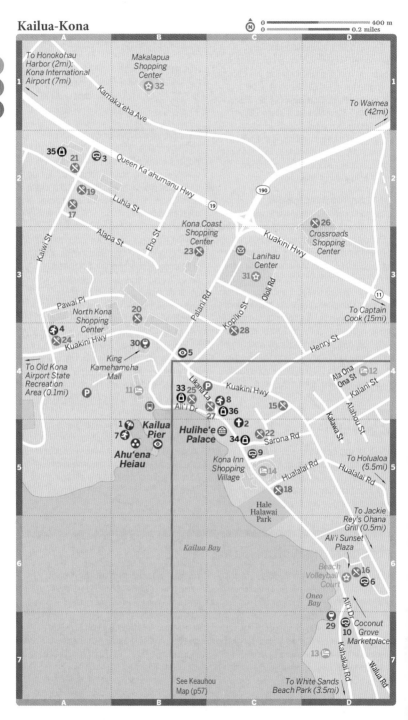

To Honokohau
Harbor (2mi);
Kona International
Airport (7mi)

Makalapua
Shopping
Center
🌟 32

To Waimea
(42mi)

Kamaka'eha Ave

35 🔒 21 ☕ 3 Queen Ka'ahumanu Hwy

19 Luhia St

17

Kaiwi St Alapa St Eho St

Kona Coast
Shopping
Center
23

190

19

Kuakini Hwy

Crossroads
Shopping
Center
26

Lanihau
Center

Palani Rd

31 🌟

Ololi Rd

To Captain
Cook (15mi)

11

Pawai Pl
North Kona
Shopping
Center

4
24

Kuakini Hwy

20

King
Kamehameha
Mall

30

Kopiko St

28

5

Henry St

To Old Kona
Airport State
Recreation
Area (0.1mi)

P

11 🏪

🚌

Kuakini Hwy

33 🔒 25
Ali'i Dr 27

Likana La P

8
36

15

Ala Ona
Ona St 12

Kalani St

Kalawa St

Alahou St

To Holualoa
(5.5mi)

1 🏛
7

Kailua
Pier

Ahu'ena
Heiau

Hulihe'e 🏛
Palace

2

34 🔒

22

Sarona Rd

9

Kona Inn
Shopping
Village

14

18

Hale
Halawai
Park

Hualalai Rd

To Jackie
Rey's Ohana
Grill (0.5mi)

Ali'i Sunset
Plaza

Kailua Bay

Beach
Volleyball
Court

16

6

Oneo
Bay

Ali'i Dr

29

Coconut
Grove
Marketplace

10

13

Kahakai Rd

Wailua Rd

See Keauhou
Map (p57)

To White Sands
Beach Park (3.5mi)

Kailua-Kona

Admission to the palace includes a 40-minute tour, which provides interesting anecdotes about past royal occupants – including corpulent Princess Ruth who lived in a grass shack because she couldn't make it up the koa stairs! The Kona Historical Society **walking tour** (p43), which comes to the palace, includes admission.

The **concert series** (admission free; ⊙4pm, 3rd Sun each month) held here is a treat, with Hawaiian music and hula performed on the grass facing sparkling Kailua Bay.

MOKU'AIKAUA CHURCH　　Church
(☎329-0655; www.mokuaikaua.org; 75-5713 Ali'i Dr; ⊙dawn-dusk) When the first Christian missionaries landed in Kailua Bay on April 4, 1820, their timing couldn't have been better. King Liholiho had abolished the traditional religion on that very spot just a few months before. He gave the missionaires the site, just a few minutes' walk from Kamehameha's Ahu'ena Heiau, to establish Hawai'i's first Christian church.

Completed in 1836, Moku'aikaua Church matches its island setting, with walls of lava rock held together by a mortar of sand and coral lime. The posts and beams, hewn with stone adzes and smoothed down with chunks of coral, are made from resilient ohia, and the pews and pulpit are made of koa, the most prized native hardwood. The steeple tops out at 112ft, making the church the tallest structure in Kailua-Kona.

The church holds **contemporary services** (🕑9am Sun) and **traditional services** (🕑11am Sun) featuring the Ohana Choir and are followed by a short lecture on the history of the church.

KAILUA PIER   Landmark

Kailua Bay was once a major cattle-shipping area, where the animals were stampeded into the water and forced to swim out to steamers waiting to transport them to Honolulu slaughterhouses. Today, the pier and bay are jumping with workers swimming on their lunch hour and canoe clubs blessing their vessels.

The annual International Billfish Tournament kicks off here with cries of 'Start fishing! Start fishing! Start fishing!', continuing the sportfishing tradition launched in 1915 when the pier was built. Kailua Pier also marks the start and finish of the Ironman Triathlon World Championship, is the dock for cruise ships, and serves dive and cruise boats.

The pier is located at the western end of Ali'i Dr, directly in front of King Kamehameha's Kona Beach Hotel.

AHU'ENA HEIAU   Temple
(near King Kamehameha's Kona Beach Hotel)

After uniting the Hawaiian islands, Kamehameha the Great established his kingdom's royal court in Lahaina on Maui, but he continued to use Ahu'ena Heiau as his personal retreat and temple. He died here in May 1819 and it was here his body was prepared for burial; though, in keeping with tradition, his bones were secreted elsewhere, hidden so securely no one has ever found them (though some theories point to **Kaloko Fishpond**; see p93). Notice the towering carved *ki'i* (god) image with a golden plover on top of the temple: these long-distance flyers may have guided the first Polynesians to Hawaii.

TOP CHOICE KONA CLOUD FOREST SANCTUARY   Nature Reserve

(www.konacloudforest.com) Escape the heat and head upland to Kaloko Mauka, a subdivision containing a spectacular

Kona Cloud Forest Sanctuary

botanical ecosystem unknown even to most locals. The sanctuary is a privately owned 70-acre collection of plant species, both native (such as koa, ohia and *hapu'u*) and introduced (including spectacular palms, bromeliads, orchids, ferns and bamboo) from around the world. At 3000ft above sea level, the climate is cool and moist; here plants absorb moisture not only from rain (as in rainforests) but from mist and clouds.

Norm Bezona, the sanctuary director, is an expert on tropical horticulture and sustainable agriculture. Much of the Kaloko Mauka subdivision has already been destroyed, but Bezona helped to establish a tax break for property owners who maintain their forestland instead of clearing it. When he leads tours for school kids, he asks them for a moment of silence to hear the birds, insects and other forest sounds in the vast, often-unseen ecological web.

 # Activities

With rocky shores and rough waters, Kailua-Kona isn't ideal for swimming – for that head north to Kekaha Kai State Park or Hapuna Beach State Recreation Area. Still, Kahalu'u Beach Park is a good bet when calm, as is Old Kona Airport – especially with kids. Note that snorkeling cruises only launch from Kailua-Kona; the actual snorkeling is done in North or South Kona's glassily calm waters.

Bodyboarding & Surfing

White Sands Beach Park is a favorite spot for bodyboarding, while board surfers like Banyans' **Kahalu'u Beach Park** (near the banyan tree north of White Sands Beach Park) and **Pine Trees**, near Wawaloli (OTEC) Beach.

PACIFIC VIBRATIONS   Surfing
(329-4140; pacvibe@hawaii.rr.com; 75-5702 Likana Lane; 10am-5:30pm Mon-Fri, to 3:30pm Sat) The first surf shop in West Hawai'i provides board rentals and expert advice.

Diving

The Kona Coast is known for calm, clear waters, unique lava formations and coral reefs. Near the shore, divers can see steep drop-offs with lava tubes, caves and diverse marine life. In deeper waters there are 40 popular boat-dive areas, including an **airplane wreck** off Keahole Point.

A signature experience is a **night dive** with Pacific manta rays. These gentle giants, with wingspans of 8ft to an amazing 20ft, will leave you speechless and wearing a shit-eating grin. If you're certified but rusty, the two-tank dive allows time to practice during the first afternoon dive (especially if it's your first night dive). Afternoon dives are generally mundane, with day fish settling into hiding places and night fish not yet out. Manta ray sightings are not guaranteed, no matter what dive operators promise. Some operators (eg Fair Wind and Sea Paradise) will let you repeat the cruise for free if none are sighted.

Check the **Manta Pacific Research Foundation** (www.mantapacific.org) website for manta sighting data and guidelines for responsible manta watching. And bring your own dive light and let them come to you!

Most dive tours launch from **Honokohau Harbor** (map p90) but have their bricks-and-mortar location in Kailua-Kona. Including all gear, the cost of a standard two-tank dive ranges from $100 to $140 and one-tank night dives to see manta rays cost between $100 and $145. PADI Open Water certification programs cost about $500.

JACK'S DIVING LOCKER   Diving
(329-7585, 800-345-4807; www.jacks divinglocker.com; Coconut Grove Marketplace, 75-5813 Ali'i Dr; 8am-8pm daily, until 6pm Sun) One of the best outfits for introductory dives and courses, with extensive programs for kids. Housed at a 5000ft-deep facility, with a store, classrooms, tank room and 12ft-deep dive pool. Offers boat and shore dives, as well as night manta-ray dives; snorkelers welcome on many trips. Its five boats (from 23ft to 46ft) handle

groups of six to 18 divers; obviously the smaller the group and more experienced the guide, the more rewarding the trip. In 2005, Jack's received a statewide Living Reef Award for helping to protect Hawaii's coral reefs from anchor damage.

SANDWICH ISLE DIVERS   Diving
(☎ 329-9188, 888-743-3483; www.sandwichisle divers.com; Kona Marketplace, 75-5729 Ali'i Dr) Small outfit run by a husband-and-wife team offers trips that feel personalized due to a six-person maximum and captain's marine biology degree. These folks have decades of experience in Kona waters.

Big Island Divers   Diving
(☎ 329-6068; www.bigislanddivers.com; 74-5467 Kaiwi St) Personable staff with expansive shop; all boat dives are open to snorkelers. Specializes in night and manta dives, including black night dives.

Fishing

Kailua-Kona is legendary for big-game fishing, so it's no surprise that over 100 charter boats are available to take you aboard. The standard cost for joining an existing party starts at $80 per person for a half-day (four-hour) trip. If you charter a whole boat, you can take up to six people for $450 to $600 for a half-day and between $750 and $3500 for a full day, depending on the boat. Ask whether the captain shares the catch.

Agencies book for so many boats that it's impossible to guarantee quality or consistency, but **Charter Desk** (☎ 326-1800, 888-566-2487; www.charterdesk.com; ⏰6am-6pm) is reputable and can match you with 60 boats. Use smaller **Charter Services Hawaii** (☎ 800-567-2650; www. konazone.com) if Charter Desk is booked up.

Highly recommended boats include the following:

Captain Jeff's Charters   Fishing
(☎ 895-1852; www.fishinkona.com; exclusive 6hr charter $550-750) Longtime captain is a straight shooter who offers tailored trips, insider advice and a share of the catch. Informative website.

Hooked Up Sportfishing Fishing

(☎960-5877; www.konacharterboat.com; exclusive 4hr charter $400) Personalized, family-oriented service on a 42ft boat with a proven catch record.

Sea Wife II Fishing

(☎888-329-1806; www.seawifecharters.com; shared charter per person $95, exclusive 4hr charter $550) Go here to join a shared charter. Nonfishing tagalongs cost $50.

Kayak Fishing

Once again, the Big Island is big on the newest watersport adventure: kayak fishing. Imagine landing a 25lb *ahi* (yellowfin tuna) or 35lb *ono* (wahoo) from a kayak – but not without a fight! A couple of professional, licensed outfitters can hook you up to do exactly that (OK, your catch

Island Insights

The largest Pacific blue marlin (1376lb) was caught in Kailua-Kona on May 31, 1982, by angler Jay de Beaubien. If you can't visualize the size of a 1-ton 'grander,' go to King Kamehameha's Kona Beach Hotel to see the mounted 1993 Hawaiian International Billfish Tournament Pro-Am record catch, a 1166lb marlin, and the 1986 record catch weighing in at 1065lb. Read all about the latest, greatest catches in the official state record keeper *Hawaii Fishing News* (www.hawaiifishingnews.com).

might not weigh 25lb...). No experience is necessary and, due to the nature of the sport, tours are usually just you and your guide.

For fully guided tours and all gear, we recommend the following:

Lucky Gecko Kayak Fishing Kayak Fishing
(☎557-9827; www.luckygeckokayakfishing.com; leaves from Keauhou Bay; 5hr tour $125)

Kayak Fishing Hawai'i Kayak Fishing
(☎936-4400; www.kayakfishinghawaii.com; 6hr tour $250) Based in Kawaihae but travels island-wide.

Outrigger Canoeing

It has been years in the making, but visitors can finally try their hand at traditional outrigger canoeing thanks to the friendly folks at the **Kona Boys Beach Shack** (minimum 2 people, adult/child $50/25) at Kamakahonu Beach. Feel what the original Polynesian settlers must have felt with the water rushing under their hull as they approached the volcanic shores of the Big Island, with celebrated Hawaiian paddler Uncle Jesse as your guide.

To see how the pros do it, check out the January to May race schedule of the **Hawai'i Island Paddlesports Association** (www.kaikahoe.org). And don't miss the **Queen Lili'uokalani Canoe Race** (www.kaiopua.org) on the Labor Day weekend.

Snorkeling

For easy-access snorkeling, Kahalu'u Beach Park is your closest and best option. For snorkeling further afield, take a cruise from Keauhou Pier or Honokohau Harbor (p43).

Snorkel Bob's Snorkeling
(☎329-0770; www.snorkelbob.com; 75-5831 Kahakai Rd; ◷8am-5pm) Offers gear rental; near the Royal Kona Resort.

Snuba

For non–scuba divers, snuba can be a fun option. You can descend 25ft underwater using a breathing hose attached to a raft and your air tank.

SNUBA BIG ISLAND Snuba
(☎326-7446; www.snubabigisland.com) Offers daily **beach dives** (1½hr tour $89; ◷departs 9am, 11am, 1pm & 3pm), leaving from Kailua Pier, and **boat dives** (3hr tour & 1/2 dives $145/170; ◷departs 8:30am & 12:30pm), leaving from Honokohau Harbor. Minimum age is eight, but kids as young as four can participate by wearing a flotation device and staying at the surface.

Stand Up Paddling

There are three new crazes on the Big Island: kayak fishing, Zumba and stand up paddling (SUP). Each gets you moving, but only SUP (see boxed text, p333) delivers a core workout in the company of dolphins,

Palm trees, Kailua-Kona beach
PHOTOGRAPHER: © MACDUFF EVERTON/CORBIS

turtles and tropical fish. And the best part is anyone can do it – even the less fit among us can groove to the ease and fun of SUP.

KONA BOYS BEACH
SHACK   Stand Up Paddling
(329-2345; www.konaboys.com; 90min lesson $75, 1hr rental $25; 8am-5pm) Offers lessons and rents gear; right on Kamakahonu Beach.

Yoga

Kona Yoga   Yoga
(331-1310; www.konayoga.com; Sunset Shopping Plaza, 77-6425 Hwy 11; drop-in class $15) A no-frills studio with a limited schedule. Owner Barbara Uechi teaches Iyengar-inspired classes with lots of care and humor. Acupuncture and massage are also available.

Bikram Yoga Kona   Yoga
(443-9990; www.bikramkona.com; Kuakini Center, 74-5563 Kaiwi St; drop-in class $16) Those who like it hot should drop into the island's only Bikram studio.

 Tours

BODY GLOVE HISTORICAL
SUNSET DINNER CRUISE   Cruise
(800-551-8911; www.bodyglovehawaii.com; 75-5629 Kuakini Hwy; adult/child 6-17/child 5 & under $94/58/free; historical cruise 4pm Tue, Thu & Sat, cocktail cruise 5:30pm Wed & Fri) Popular historical cruises along the Kona Coast last three hours and include dinner, kickin' live music and a fascinating historical narration. The sunset 'booze' cruise lasts two hours and features an open bar. The boat is wheelchair accessible.

KONA BREWING
COMPANY   Brewery Tour
(334-2739; www.konabrewingco.com; North Kona Shopping Center, 75-5629 Kuakini Hwy; admission free; tours 10:30am & 3pm Mon-Fri) Since opening in 1994, this company has been Hawai'i's mainstay in the micro-brewery phenomenon. The once-small, family-run operation is now one of the nation's fastest-growing microbreweries – from Maine to California you can sip 'liquid

Where do you go on your day off? I like Magic Sands right in town. It's a local favorite for people watching and bodysurfing. In the winter, it gets a little rough and loses some of its sand; it's better in summer. My favorite all-round beach is Hapuna (p118) – phenomenal.

What do you recommend for travelers with kids? The Fair Wind Snorkel Cruise (p45) to Kealakekua Bay is great. The crew is fun and kids love jumping off the upper deck or riding the slide into the bay. They always have fun sea toys that make you feel safe while snorkeling.

Let's talk fish. Tell us something we don't know. The Big Island has amazing fishing grounds right off the coast – it's the best of all the Hawaiian islands for fresh fish. The KTA Super Stores (p49) on Palani Rd has the best fish counter. Top quality, nothing is ever frozen – this is the real deal. Try the *poke*. For sushi, I like Sushi Shiono (p49), owned by a Japanese businessman who wants guaranteed good sushi when he's on the island.

Your restaurant is on the official Ironman route. What tips do you have for fans? Watch the swim portion from Kailua Pier and then come up here to watch the cycling leg – we set up lawn chairs in the parking lot. They go up at 25 mph and then whiz back down again at 45 mph, so it's twice the fun. The finish line is also a blast. Cyclists can feel like an Ironman for a day by renting a top-end road bike (p55) and pedalling the official Kailua-Kona to Hawi route.

Aloha.' Tours include samples. Enter the parking lot from Kaiwi St.

KONA HISTORICAL
SOCIETY   Walking Tour
(323-3222; www.konahistorical.org; 90min tour $15) This worthwhile and informative walking tour covers historical sites in

PETER FRENCH / PHOTOLIBRARY

downtown Kailua-Kona, and includes a booklet with over 40 archival photos of historic Kailua. Tours are by appointment and have 10-person minimum.

HAWAIIAN WALKWAYS   Walking Tour
(☎800-457-7759; www.hawaiianwalkways. com; adult/child 8-12 $95/75; ☉8:30am-1pm) Offers three-hour walking tours through the Kona Cloud Forest Sanctuary; guides are knowledgeable on botany and geology, and the tour ends with a visit to the adjacent **Mountain Thunder Coffee Plantation**. Wear sturdy shoes.

For sedentary, rather than active, ocean tours, consider the following:

**ATLANTIS
SUBMARINES**   Submarine Tour
(☎329-6626, 800-548-6262; www.atlantis adventures.com; adult/child 12 & under $99/45; ☉submarine rides 10am, 11:30am & 1pm) Underwater portion of this pricey tour lasts 35 minutes. It descends 100ft into a coral crevice fronting the Royal Kona Resort and explores a couple of nearby shipwrecks. The battery-powered sub has 26 portholes and carries 48 passengers. Japanese-language headsets are available. Children must be over 36in in height.

**KAILUA BAY CHARTER
COMPANY**   Cruise
(☎324-1749; www.konaglassbottomboat.com; 50min tour adult/child 12 & under $40/20; ☉tours hourly from 10:30am) See Kailua-Kona's coastline, and its underwater reef and sea life, from a 36ft glass-bottomed boat with a pleasant crew and onboard naturalist. There's easy boarding for mobility-impaired passengers.

Snorkeling

Snorkeling cruises aren't cheap, but they offer a chance to enter deeper waters, sail along the panoramic coast and learn from longtime seamen. And what with water slides and floaty noodles, they're also great for kids. Opt for a morning departure when water conditions are best. Cruises depart from either Keauhou Pier or Honokohau Harbor. Book online for frequent discounts.

Most tours head south to Kealakekua Bay, but other coves, like more northerly Pawai Bay, can be just as scenic and less crowded. The coast south of Kailua-Kona features beautiful lava cliffs and caves, while the northern coast is a flat lava shelf with lots of marine life.

There are two types of cruises. Zodiac rafts are zippy and thrilling, capable of exploring sea caves, lava tubes and blowholes, but you must expect a bumpy ride and no shade or toilets. Catamarans are much larger, smoother and comfier but can't go as close into coves as the rafts can. Most diving outfits allow snorkelers aboard for $80 to $95.

Zodiac Tours

TOP CHOICE **SEA QUEST** — Snorkeling
(☎ 329-7238, 888-732-2283; www.seaquesthawaii; Keauhou Bay; 1-snorkel cruise adult/child 5-12 $72/62, 2-snorkel cruise adult/child 5-12 $92/75, whale-watching cruise adult/child 5-12 $72/62) Sea Quest has four rigid-hull inflatable rafts that take up to six or 14 passengers. On offer are one- and two-stop snorkel adventures, plus whale-watching cruises. All snorkel cruises visit Kealakekua Bay, with Honaunau Bay (Two-Step) serving as the second stop.

Captain Zodiac — Snorkeling
(☎ 329-3199; www.captainzodiac.com; Honokohau Harbor; half-day cruise adult/child 4-12 $100/84) In business since 1974, Captain Zodiac makes daily trips to Kealakekua Bay in 24ft rigid-hull inflatable rafts with up to 16 passengers and a jaunty pirate theme.

Catamaran Tours

TOP CHOICE **SEA PARADISE** — Snorkeling
(☎ 322-2500, 800-322-5662; www.seaparadise.com; Keauhou Bay; adult/child 4-12 snorkel cruise incl 2 meals $99/59, manta snorkel $89/59, 2-tank dive $145, manta dive $110) This highly recommended outfit offers morning snorkel cruises to Kealakekua Bay, dive trips (including a bargain-priced manta ray night dive) and sunset dinner cruises on a 46ft catamaran with a friendly, professional crew.

KAMANU CHARTERS — Snorkeling
(☎ 329-2021, 800-348-3091; www.kamanu.com; Honokohau Harbor; adult/child 12 & under $90/50) Snorkel in quiet Pawai Bay, just north of the protected waters of the Old Kona Airport State Recreation Area. The 36ft catamaran, which motors to the bay and sails back, maxes out at 24 people. Kamanu does a

The Best...
Kailua-Kona for Kids

1 Surf lessons, Kahalu'u Beach Park (p56)

2 Keiki Center, Sheraton Keauhou Bay Resort & Spa (p61)

3 Premium ice cream, Ali'i Dr (p50)

4 Kona Cloud Forest Sanctuary (p38)

night manta snorkel ($80), and the boat can be privately chartered.

FAIR WIND — Snorkeling
(☎ 345-0268, 800-677-9461; www.fair-wind.com; Keauhou Bay; morning snorkel adult/child 4-12/child 3 & under $125/75/29, afternoon snorkel adult/child 4-12 $109/69) The *Fair Wind II,* a scrappy 100-passenger catamaran with two 15ft slides, sails daily to Kealakekua Bay. Cruises on the luxury hydrofoil catamaran *Hula Kai* are longer and explore less-trafficked waters; minimum age is seven (per person including meal $165). Divers are welcome. The manta ray snorkel is hugely popular and can crowd out others.

Whale Watching

Although snorkeling, diving and fishing tours often also offer whale watching during humpback season (December to April), you are more likely to see, and learn, more on specialized tours.

TOP CHOICE **DAN MCSWEENEY'S WHALE WATCH LEARNING ADVENTURES** — Whale Watching
(☎ 322-0028, 888-942-5376; www.ilovewhales.com; 3hr cruise adult/child $80/70; ⏰ Jul, Aug & Nov-Apr) We recommend marine-mammal biologist Dan McSweeney's excursions. His tours are not just a seasonal add-on but focus on whale sightings and education. In other words, whales are the main

45

event! Several other types of whales and five species of dolphin can also be seen in Kona waters year-round. Hydrophones allow passengers to hear whale songs.

 ## Festivals & Events

KONA BREWERS FESTIVAL   *Festival*

(📞331-3033, 334-1884; www.konabrewers festival.com; admission $50) On the second Saturday in March, Kona Brewing Company throws an annual beer tasting festival to promote Hawaii's microbrew industry. Taste 30 craft beers plus gourmet eats from scores of local restaurants. Proceeds go to environmental and children's groups. Book in advance.

HAWAIIAN INTERNATIONAL BILLFISH TOURNAMENT   *Competition*

(📞836-3422; www.hibtfishing.com) Hawaii's most prestigious sportfishing competition, with five days of all-day fishing followed by weigh-ins and other festivities at Kailua Pier. The tourney starts in late July or early August.

IRONMAN TRIATHLON WORLD CHAMPIONSHIP   *Competition*

(📞329-0063; www.ironman.com) On the second Saturday in October, all traffic halts for this premier endurance test that finishes on Ali'i Dr; see p47.

KONA COFFEE CULTURAL FESTIVAL   *Festival*

(📞326-7820; www.konacoffeefest.com; admission $3, additional fees for selected events) For 10 days during the early November harvest season, the community celebrates the Kona coffee pioneers and their renowned beans. The dozens of events include a cupping competition, a recipe contest, art exhibits, farm tours, coffee tastings and a coffee-picking contest.

Sleeping

The quality of hotels and condos along Ali'i Dr in the walkable center of Kailua-Kona is only fair to middling. More attractive offerings are just outside town (in all directions). Since convenience is a siren song, reservations for all Kailua properties are recommended in high season.

Coffee-picking contest

Men of Steel, Women of Titanium

When thousands of athletes and fans swoop into Kailua-Kona each October, locals gripe about traffic and crowds. But nobody can deny the awesome spectacle of the **Ironman Triathlon World Championship** (www.ironman.com). The granddaddy of triathlons is a grueling combination of a 2.4-mile ocean swim, 112-mile bike race and 26.2-mile run. And it has to be done in 17 hours. Belgian Luc Van Lierde set the current men's record at eight hours and four minutes in 1996, while Chrissie Wellington of Great Britain set the women's record at eight hours, 54 minutes and two seconds in 2002.

Harsh conditions make the event the ultimate endurance test. Heat bouncing off the lava commonly exceeds 100°F, making dehydration and heat exhaustion major challenges. Many contenders arrive on the island weeks before to acclimatize. On race day, over 5500 volunteers line the 140-mile course to hand out 26,000 gallons of fluid to the world's toughest athletes pushed to the max – who, in the past, have included a 76-year-old nun, an Iraq war veteran amputee, and father–son Team Hoyt, with Rick pushing son Dick in a wheelchair; these guys are six-time Ironmen!

Begun in 1978 by Navy SEALS on a dare, the Ironman was labeled 'lunatic' by *Sports Illustrated*. A few years later, the lead athlete crawled to the finish line, losing by seconds. With that drama, the sports world was hooked. Today the event draws up to 2000 athletes from over 50 countries. Whaddya win if you win? Who cares? It's all about the challenge (and the bragging rights).

To snag the best deals on condos and vacation rentals – the best bets for families – check a variety of sources, including **Vacation Rental by Owner** (www.vrbo.com) and **Alternative Hawaii** (www.alternative-hawaii.com).

B&Bs, Inns & Hostels

Parking is no problem at the following. Most places have a three-night minimum stay.

TOP CHOICE **PLUMERIA HOUSE**　Inn $$
(☎326-9255; www.plumeriahouse.com; Kilohana St; 1br $80-120; @) Shh, this immaculate 800-sq-ft one-bedroom deal is a downright steal for longer stays (four-night minimum). Located in the upland Kaloko residential neighborhood, the unit features many convenient touches: full kitchen, filtered water, patio tables and use of washer-dryer. Wheelchair accessible; $50 cleaning fee.

KONA SUGAR SHACK　Inn $$
(☎895-2203, 877-324-6444; www.konasugarshack.com; 77-6483 Ali'i Dr; r $140-500; P ❄ 🛜 ♨ 🛗) Your friendly, artistic hosts have created an attractively funky, yet homey, shack (really a B&B without breakfast), mostly solar powered, with shared outdoor kitchen, a miniscule pool, eclectic furnishings and lots of amenities. Also, they love kids. The location almost directly across from White Sands Beach is sweet. The entire house, sleeping 15, is available for rent.

KOA WOOD HALE INN/ PATEY'S PLACE　Hostel $
(☎329-9663; www.alternative-hawaii.com/affordable/kona.htm; 75-184 Ala Ona Ona St; dm/s/d from $25/55/65; @ 🛜) This well-managed hostel is Kailua-Kona's best budget deal, offering basic, quiet and clean dorms and private rooms (all with shared baths, kitchens and living rooms) on a residential street that's walking distance to Ali'i Dr. A fully equipped,

47

two-bedroom apartment is also available ($130; maximum five people). Travelers young and old create a friendly, low-key vibe. No drugs, alcohol or shoes indoors.

1ST CLASS B&B B&B $$
(☎329-8778, 888-769-1110; www.dolbandb.com; 77-6504 Kilohana St; studio/cottage incl breakfast $165/175; ☎) It's rather like staying at grandma's house, if she had two airy independent units overlooking panoramic Kailua Bay. The studio and cottage are well furnished, immaculate and share a lanai with ocean views, but are rather pricey. Longtime resident Dolores offers a hot breakfast, from Belgian waffles to frittatas.

A number of stellar places to stay are located several miles upland, on the cool slopes of Mt Hualalai, including:

Nancy's Hideaway B&B $$
(☎325-3132, 866-325-3132; www.nancyshideaway.com; 73-1530 Uanani Pl; studio/cottage incl breakfast $130/150; ☎) A peaceful retreat, 6 miles upslope from town with a freestanding studio or one-bedroom cottage, each clean and contemporary, with kitchenette. No young kids.

Honu Kai B&B B&B $$
(☎329-8676; www.honukaibnb.com; 74-1529 Hao Kuni St; d incl breakfast $150-195; @ ☎) A plush, upscale four-room B&B, with rich fabrics, carved bed frames and Asian and Hawaiian decor. A separate cottage has full kitchen. There are shared gardens, Jacuzzi, and rooftop lanai here.

Hotels & Resorts

Although centrally located and close to the ocean, Kailua-Kona doesn't have the best selection of hotels. Book online to save big-time.

KING KAMEHAMEHA'S KONA BEACH HOTEL Hotel $$
(☎329-2911, reservations 800-367-2111; www.konabeachhotel.com; 75-5660 Palani Rd; r $170-230; P ❄ ☎ ☲) Location and spiffy renovation are the watchwords for the historic 'King Kam' anchoring Ali'i Dr. Chic room decor, a new Herb Kawainui Kane exhibit in the lobby (open to nonguests) and free in-room wi-fi are all draws here. Walk to

recommended restaurants or hop over to the Kona Boys Beach Shack to try stand up paddling or sea kayaking.

ROYAL KONA RESORT Resort $$$
(☎329-3111, reservations 800-222-5642; www.royalkona.com; 75-5852 Ali'i Dr; r $180-265, ste $210-330; P ❄ @ ☲) Spread over three striking towers, the Royal Kona has a breezy, open-air feel. Surrounded by a tropical theme and Don's Mai Tai Bar, you'll know you're in Hawaii. Although all rooms have been remodeled, those in the pricier Ali'i and Lagoon Towers are nicest and biggest. A protected, saltwater lagoon is perfect for kids. Check out the long menu of services at the **Lotus Center Spa** (www.konaspa.com), located at the resort.

Uncle Billy's Kona Bay Hotel Hotel $$
(☎329-1393, 800-367-5102; www.unclebilly.com; 75-5744 Ali'i Dr; r $95-120; P ❄ ☎ ☲) In a pinch, head to this hotel. The good: downtown location and lots of amenities like a pool. The bad: too much street noise and frumpy interior.

Condos

Families and DIYers will be happiest in a condo where you can cook, romp, and come and go as you please. Condos are also money savers if you stay a week or longer and most provide free parking – bonus! Remember, though, that individual units vary in quality and style and in Kailua-Kona 'oceanfront' doesn't mean beach since there's so little sand. The best selection of condos is on the southern part of Ali'i Dr near Keauhou.

Most Kailua-Kona condos (and vacation rentals) retain a primary management firm for bookings. Check with the following rental agencies, which operate mainly by phone and internet:

ATR Properties (☎329-6020, 888-311-6020; www.konacondo.com)

Elite Property Network (☎329-7977, 800-358-7977; www.hawaii-kona.com)

Hawaii Resort Management (☎329-3333, 800-244-4752; www.konahawaii.com)

SunQuest Vacations & Property Management Hawaii (☎329-6438, 800-367-5168; www.sunquest-hawaii.com)

West Hawaii Properties (334-1199, 800-799-5662; www.konarentals.com)

Eating

If there's one thing Kailua-Kona is good for, it's satisfying cravings for good food. You don't have to spend a lot here to dine on *'ono kine grinds* (good food) – you just to need to know where to go.

TOP CHOICE **KANAKA KAVA** Hawaiian **$$**
(www.kanakakava.com; Coconut Grove Marketplace, 75-5803 Ali'i Dr; à la carte $4-6, mains $14-16; ⏱10am-10pm, to 11pm Thu-Sat) This tiny, tropical cafe is the perfect place to try kava (the mildly sedative juice of the *'awa* plant), grown by owner and chef Zachary Gibson. His delicious organic salads are topped with a choice of fish, shellfish, chicken, tofu or *poke* (cubed raw fish marinated in soy sauce, oil and chili pepper). The *kalua* pork is phenomenal. Cash only.

TOP CHOICE **JACKIE REY'S OHANA GRILL** Hawaii Regional **$$**
(www.jackiereys.com; Pottery Tce, 75-5995 Kuakini Hwy; lunch $11-15, dinner $14-28; ⏱lunch 11am-5pm Mon-Fri, dinner 5-9pm daily; 🚶) Jackie Rey's is a casual, family-owned grill with Polynesian flair and a fun retro Hawaii vibe. Yummy fare including glazed short ribs, wasabi-seared ahi and killer fresh fish tacos is served with aloha. Locals, tourists, kids, aunties – everyone loves it here. Pop in on a weekday between 2pm and 5pm for half-priced *pupu* (appetizers).

RAPANUI ISLAND CAFÉ
Island Contemporary **$$**
(Banyan Court mall, 75-5695 Ali'i Dr; lunch $6-10, dinner $10-16; ⏱11am-2pm & 5-9pm Mon-Fri, 5-9pm Sat) The New Zealand owners know curry, which they prepare with a delicious

tongue-tingly warmth. Choose from various satays, spiced pork, seafood and salads. Order the house coconut rice and wash it down with lemongrass ginger tea or a New Zealand wine.

ISLAND LAVA JAVA Cafe **$$**
(www.islandlavajavakona.com; Ali'i Sunset Plaza, 75-5799 Ali'i Dr; meals $9-18; ⏱6:30am-9:30pm; @ 🛜 🚶) This cafe is a favorite gathering spot for a sunny breakfast, leisurely dinner or Sunday brunch with almost oceanside dining on the outdoor patio. The food aims for upscale diner; if it sometimes hits closer to greasy spoon, no one minds – especially since the coffee is 100% Kona, and the beef and chicken are Big Island–raised. Portions are huge; baked goods are sinful.

ORCHID THAI Thai **$$**
(Kuakini Center, 74-5555 Kaiwi St; lunch specials $10, dinner $10-16; ⏱11:30am-3pm & 5-9pm Mon-Sat; 🚶) This neighborhood stalwart is where locals seek their curry fix. The classic preparations are handled well and without fuss. Strip mall location, but fake

Kalua pork, Kanaka Kava
GREG ELMS / LONELY PLANET IMAGES ©

Cool Scoops

For scrumptious premium ice cream (made by Kailua-Kona's own Big Island Ice Cream company), try two shops on Ali'i Dr. A modern, sparkling-clean shop, **Kope Lani** (www.kopelani.com; 75-5719 Ali'i Dr; ☺7am-9pm) is a coffee retailer with a cheery counter selling the most flavors in town. Pull up at a patio table and watch Ali'i Dr go by. Follow your nose to **Scandinavian Shave Ice Internet Café** (☎331-1626; 75-5699 Ali'i Dr; single scoop $3.50; ☺8am-9pm), which constantly exudes the soothing aroma of fresh-baked waffle cones. It also makes shave ice and offers a thrilling 45 flavors.

brick and eggplant-colored curtains warm up the interior. Bring your own alcohol.

BA-LE KONA   Vietnamese $$
(Kona Coast Shopping Center, 74-5588 Palani Rd; sandwiches $4-7, soups & plates $9-13; ☺10am-9pm Mon-Sat, 11am-7pm Sun; ☑) Come for light and healthy Vietnamese fare, not the no-frills decor and mall setting. Ba-Le offers generous, family-sized plates of the classics, from green papaya salad topped with shrimp to steaming *pho* noodle soups (with mushroom broth instead of beef broth for vegetarians).

YOU MAKE THE ROLL   Sushi $
(Kona Marketplace, 75-5725 Ali'i Dr; sushi rolls $5-7; ☺11am-7pm Mon-Fri, to 4pm Sat) Crazy combinations and low prices make this hidden sushi stand a hit with local teens and surfers. For value, not gourmet, sushi, this is it.

KILLER TACOS   Mexican $
(74-5483 Kaiwi St; mains $3-8; ☺10am-8pm Mon-Fri, to 6pm Sat; ☎) Ever wonder where all the locals and surfers chow down after a day of work and play? Look no further. The burritos are a better bang for your buck than the tacos, but everything here

is made tasty to order. Request additional hot sauce – the salsa is anemic.

KONA BREWING COMPANY   Pub $$
(☎334-2739; www.konabrewingco.com; 75-5629 Kuakini Hwy; sandwiches & salads $11-16, pizzas $15-26; ☺11am-9pm Sun-Thu, to 10pm Fri & Sat) Expect a madhouse crowd at this sprawling brewpub, despite the poorly lit outdoor seating and lackadaisical wait staff. Everyone's here for delectable Greek, spinach and Caesar salads and hand-crafted beer made on-site. Pizza toppings verge on the gourmet, but crusts are soggy and doughy. The certified organic and solar-powered-brewed beers here earn green points with the ecocrowd. Enter the parking lot from Kaiwi St.

BIG ISLAND GRILL   Diner $$
(75-5702 Kuakini Hwy; plate lunches $10, mains $10-19; ☺7:30am-9pm Mon-Sat) Big appetites are no match for the big portions served at this Denny's-style diner. The food is down-home rather than upscale, and favorites include teriyaki beef, grilled mahimahi, and giant burgers and pancakes. Friendly service can slip during busy periods.

LA BOURGOGNE   French $$$
(☎329-6711; Kuakini Plaza, 77-6400 Nalani St, at Hwy 11; mains $28-38; ☺6-10pm Tue-Sat) A dining room with no windows let alone a view? Yes, but that's the appeal of this intimate French restaurant, where slow, lingering meals are encouraged. Highly recommended is the fresh catch in a steaming crock of bouillabaisse; meat eaters, don't miss the outstanding rack of lamb. For an hour or three, you'll swear you're in France, even though you're just under 4 miles southeast from Kailua-Kona via Hwy 11.

Sushi Shiono   Japanese $
(www.sushishiono.com; Ali'i Sunset Plaza, 75-5799 Ali'i Dr; sushi & rolls $4-12; ☺lunch Mon-Fri, dinner daily) Awesomely fresh fish complemented by nice sake list.

Basik Acai   Health Food $
(www.basikacai.com; 75-5831 Kahakai Rd; bowls $6-11; ☺8am-4pm Mon-Sat; ☎☑) Healthy, wholesome bowls bursting with goodness (granola, tropical fruit, nuts) are

blended with acai for added punch. We also love this place for their use of Sustainable Island Products for take-out orders, dedication to using organic, local ingredients and composting policy. Nice ocean views from up here.

Tex Drive-In　　　　　　　Drive-in $
(Kopiko Plaza, Kopiko St; 🍴) Sinful *malasadas* (Portuguese fried dough) now available at this new outpost of the famous Honoka'a drive in, plus (wait for it!) vegetarian *loco moco*.

For fresh fruit and vegetables visit the markets, and find supermarkets at the malls:

Kona Farmers Market　　　　Market
(cnr Kaiwi & Luhia Sts; ⊘7am-5pm Sat, to 3pm Sun) An unassuming gathering, focused on local produce.

Kailua Village Farmers Market　Market
(www.konafarmersmarket.com; cnr Ali'i Dr & Hualalai Rd; ⊘7am-4pm Wed-Sun) Sells produce amid phony shell jewelry and pseudo-Hawaiian knickknacks.

Island Naturals　　　　　Health Food
(📞326-1122; www.islandnaturals.com; 74-5487 Kaiwi St; ⊘7:30am-8pm Mon-Sat, 9am-7pm Sun; 🍴) Good deli, wine selection and hot and cold bar for food on the go.

Ice shave

Kona Natural Foods　　　　Health Food
(📞329-2296; www.konanaturalfoods.net; Crossroads Shopping Center, 75-1027 Henry St; ⊘8:30am-9pm Mon-Sat, to 7pm Sun, deli to 4pm daily; 🍴) Well-stocked; decent pizza parlor attached. Safeway is also in this shopping center.

KTA Super Stores　　　　Grocery
(📞329-1677; www.ktasuperstores.com; Kona Coast Shopping Center, 74-5594 Palani Rd; ⊘5am-11pm) The Big Island's best grocery chain, featuring awesome *poke* and lots of local products.

🍷 Drinking

As you might expect, Kailua-Kona's bar scene is pretty touristy but there are a handful of places good for a cocktail or two. The Kona Brewing Company is always a good fallback.

TOP CHOICE **MIXX BISTRO**　　　　　Bar
(www.mixxbistro.com; King Kamehameha Mall, 75-5626 Kuakini Hwy; snacks $6-15; ⊘5pm-late Tue-Sat) A cool local joint, the Mixx attracts an older crowd in the early evening for wine and tapas. The younger set arrives later, especially for mojitos and salsa

dancing on Thursdays. Check the website for the live music lineup on Fridays.

HUGGO'S ON THE ROCKS
Bar

(www.huggos.com/all/rocksdefault.htm; 75-5828 Kahakai Rd; ⏰11:30am-midnight) Right on the water, with a thatched-roof bar and live music nightly, Huggo's is an ideal sunset spot. Whether it's worth staying longer depends on who's playing and who shows up. In the mornings, this place reverts to **Java on the Rocks** (⏰6-11am) with terrific coffee drinks and inventive breakfasts.

HUMPY'S BIG ISLAND ALEHOUSE
Bar

(www.humpyshawaii.com; Coconut Grove Marketplace, 75-5815 Ali'i Dr; ⏰9am-1am) Smack on the strip overlooking Kailua Bay, Humpy's would probably survive in touristy Kailua-Kona even if it didn't have over three dozen beers on tap. But fresh, foamy brews bring in the locals, giving the upstairs balcony – with its sea breeze and views – special cachet. Drop in for happy hour, weekdays 3pm to 6pm.

DON'S MAI TAI BAR
Bar

(www.royalkona.com; 75-5852 Ali'i Dr; ⏰10am-10pm) For pure kitsch, nothing beats the shameless lounge-lizard fantasy of Don's

in the Royal Kona Resort. Behold the killer ocean views with one of 10 different mai tais. Real fans roll in for the annual **Mai Tai Festival** held here each August.

Okolemaluna Tiki Bar
Bar

(www.okolemalunalounge.com; Ali'i Sunset Plaza, 75-5799 Ali'i Dr) A brand-new bar to the Kailua-Kona cocktail scene is this nearly seaside bar specializing in all manner of tropical umbrella drinks. Fruit juice mixers are fresh-squeezed.

 # Entertainment

Kailua-Kona's two hokey, cruise-ship friendly luau include a ceremony, a buffet dinner with Hawaiian specialties, an open bar and a Polynesian dinner show featuring a cast of flamboyant dancers and fire twirlers.

KBXTREME
Bowling

(☎326-2695; www.kbxtreme.com; 75-5591 Palani Rd, Lanihau Center; per hr $29, shoe rental $3; ⏰9am-midnight, bar to 2am) Poor spelling aside, Kailua-Kona's only bowling alley makes a rainy day or dull night fun. Arcade games, a full bar and diner food feature. Weekdays from 1pm to 4pm are discounted; 'cosmic bowling' happens

Sunset, Kailua-Kona

ANN CECIL / LONELY PLANET IMAGES ©

Friday and Saturday nights followed by a DJ and dancing.

King Kamehameha's Kona Beach Hotel — Luau
(☎ 329-4969; www.islandbreezeluau.com; adult/child 5-12 $74/37; ⏰ 5pm Tue, Thu & Sun) Luau benefits from a scenic oceanfront setting but crowds can reach 400. Forgo if rainy – an indoor show ain't worth it.

Stadium Cinemas — Cinema
(☎ 327-0444; Makalapua Shopping Center, 74-5469 Kamaka'eha Ave) Catch first-run movies on 10 screens.

 Shopping

Generally Kailua-Kona shopping falls into two categories: tourist traps and big-box chains. Sad but true. Target, Walmart, Circuit City, Macy's – this town has them all. The souvenir and surf shops along Ali'i Dr, including the Kailua Village Farmers Market, can be fun, but beware of 'Made in China' fakes.

TOP CHOICE BIG ISLAND JEWELERS — Jewelry
(☎ 329-8571; www.bigislandjewelers.com; 75-5695 Ali'i Dr) Family-owned and -operated for nearly four decades with master jeweler Flint Carpenter at the wheel, head here when you want an authentic Big Island keepsake (or need a ring to pop the question). The keshi natural pearl line is especially gorgeous.

NA MAKANA — Souvenirs
(☎ 326-9552; 75-5722 Likana Lane) Poke around this hole-in-the-wall for Hawaii-made souvenirs and collectibles to fit all budgets. Check out the genuine Japanese green glass fishing floats which are becoming rare. Variable opening hours epitomize 'Hawaiian time.' Pop in to Pacific Vibrations (p39) next door for surf wear.

KONA INTERNATIONAL MARKET — Souvenirs
(☎ 329-6262; www.konainternationalmarket.com; 74-5533 Luhia St; ⏰ 9am-5pm) Downsize your expectations for a worthwhile browse at this tourist-oriented marketplace. Five warehouse buildings are filled

The Best...
Kailua-Kona Sunset Spots

1 Touching down at Kona International Airport (p54)

2 Huggo's on the Rocks (p52)

3 Holuakoa Gardens & Café (p65)

4 Humpy's Big Island Alehouse (p52)

5 Kailua Pier (p38)

6 Hale Halawai Park (p35)

with cheek-by-jowl stalls selling mostly inexpensive items, such as shoes, toiletries, beach gear, flowers and island souvenirs (check the label). Ample parking, clean bathrooms, shade and a food court add to the convenience.

Crazy Shirts — Clothing
(☎ 329-2176, 800-771-2720; www.crazyshirts.com; Kona Marketplace, 75-5719 Ali'i Dr; ⏰ 9am-9pm) Once maverick, now mainstream, Crazy Shirts are worn mainly by tourists these days. The best designs feature natural dyes, such as coffee, chocolate and volcanic ash.

Sandal Bar — Shoes
(☎ 329-4290; Ali'i Sunset Plaza, 75-5799 Ali'i Dr; ⏰ 9am-9pm) Huge selection of sandals and slippers from brands such as Reef, Teva and Birkenstock.

Information

Bookstores

Kona Bay Books (☎ 326-7790; www.konabaybooks.com; 74-5487 Kaiwi St; ⏰ 10am-6pm) Awesome selection of used books, CDs and DVDs; near Kona International Market.

Now That's a Souvenir!

James and Martina Wing of **Ocean Wings Hawaii** (www.dolphindreams.com) have been swimming with the manta rays (and other spectacular Big Island marine life) for decades. Most nights, no matter which outfitter you go with, you'll meet them on the dive, filming the underwater ballet in which you and the rays star. The movie is shown in the parking lot afterwards where you can buy a professionally edited and musically scored DVD ($55) or download ($50) of your experience.

Internet Access

Island Lava Java (☎ 327-2161; Ali'i Sunset Plaza, 75-5799 Ali'i Dr; per 20min $4; ⏰ 6am-10pm) Free wi-fi with any purchase, plus two computers for paid access.

Scandinavian Shave Ice Internet Café (☎ 331-1626; 75-5699 Ali'i Dr; per hr $8; ⏰ 10am-7pm) Six computers, all with printer connections.

Internet Resources

Big Island Visitors Bureau (www.bigisland.org) Basic info with handy calendar of events.

KonaWeb (www.konaweb.com) Condo listings and reader-provided restaurant reviews, since 1995.

Media

NEWSPAPERS

Hawaii Tribune-Herald (www.hawaiitribune-herald.com) The Big Island's main daily newspaper.

West Hawaii Today (www.westhawaiitoday.com) Kona Coast's daily newspaper.

RADIO

A station guide is available at www.hawaiiradiotv.com/bigisleradio.html.

KAGB 99.1 FM (www.kaparadio.com) The Kona-side home of effervescent KAPA – Hawaii and island music.

KKUA 90.7 FM (www.hawaiipublicradio.org) Hawaii Public Radio; classical music, talk and news.

KLUA 93.9 FM Native FM (previously 'Da Beat') plays island and reggae tunes.

KMWB 93.1 Classic rock.

Medical Services

Kona Community Hospital (☎ 322-9311; www.kch.hhsc.org; 79-1019 Haukapila St, Kealakekua) Located about 10 miles south of Kailua-Kona.

Longs Drugs (☎ 329-1380; Lanihau Center, 75-5595 Palani Rd; ⏰ 8am-9pm Mon-Sat, to 6pm Sun) A centrally located drugstore and pharmacy.

Money

The following banks have 24-hour ATMs:

Bank of Hawaii (☎ 326-3900; Lanihau Center, 75-5595 Palani Rd)

First Hawaiian Bank (☎ 329-2461; Lanihau Center, 74-5593 Palani Rd)

Post

Post office (☎ 331-8307; Lanihau Center, 74-5577 Palani Rd)

🛈 Getting There & Away

Air

Kona International Airport at Keahole (KOA; ☎ 327-9520; www.hawaii.gov/koa; Queen Ka'ahumanu Hwy) Located 7 miles north of Kailua-Kona; try to avoid late-afternoon arrivals on weekdays, when the highway is jammed with commuters.

Bus

Hele-On Bus (p355) This free service runs from Kailua-Kona to Captain Cook multiple times daily (1½ hours) and to Pahala (two hours), Hilo (3½ hours) and Waimea (1½ hours). The South Kohala resorts, meanwhile, are serviced three times daily (1½ hours). All routes are serviced Monday through Saturday.

Honu Express (one-way fare $1; ⏰ 9am-8pm) Another option is this trolley running between Keauhou and Kailua-Kona with stops including Magic Sands Beach, Coconut Grove Market

Place and Kailua Pier. Anyone can ride; check the schedule at www.keauhoushoppingcenter.com or any Keauhou hotel.

Car

The drive from Kailua-Kona to Hilo (via Waimea) is 92 miles and takes 2½ hours; a bit longer via Volcano. For other driving times and distances, see p353. For car rental information, see p353.

To avoid snarly commuter traffic on Hwy 11 leading in to and away from Kailua-Kona, try the Haleki'i Bypass Rd (see p74).

Getting Around

To/From the Airport

A car is almost necessary on Hawai'i, but if you're not renting one, taxis are available at the airport from dawn to dusk; late pickups can be booked in advance. The fare averages $25 to Kailua-Kona and $45 to Waikoloa.

Speedi Shuttle (329-5433, 877-242-5777; www.speedishuttle.com) Charges between $25 and $45, depending on your destination; might be more economical for large groups. Book in advance.

Bicycle

Kailua-Kona is a bike-friendly town.

Hawaiian Pedals (329-2294; www.hawaiianpedals.com; Kona Inn Shopping Village, 75-5744 Ali'i Dr; per day $20; 9:30am-8pm) Rents well-used hybrid bikes for cruising around town.

Bike Works (326-2453; www.bikeworkskona.com; Hale Hana Center, 74-5583 Luhia St; per day $40-60; 9am-6pm Mon-Sat, 10am-4pm Sun) Affiliated with Hawaiian Pedals, rents higher-end bikes. Rentals include helmet, lock, pump and patch kit.

Bus

Hele-On Bus (p355) Stops in Kailua-Kona.

Honu Express (p62) Stops in Kailua-Kona.

Car

As soon as the sun starts heading down, Ali'i Dr in downtown Kailua-Kona gets congested. Free public parking is available in a lot between Likana Lane and Kuakini Hwy. Many of the shopping centers along Ali'i Dr have free parking lots.

Moped & Motorcycle

Doesn't it look fun zipping down Ali'i Dr on a moped? And what a breeze to park! If you want to get around town like a local, consider a rental. The official riding area is from Waikoloa up north to Captain Cook down south.

Big Island Harley Davidson (635-0542; www.hawaiiharleyrental.com; 75-5633 Palani Rd; per day/week $179/763) If you're after something a bit more...macho.

Scooter Brothers (327-1080; www.scooterbrothers.com; King Kamehameha Mall, 75-5626 Kuakini Hwy; hr/day/week $20/60/266; 10am-6pm)

Hats, Kimura Lauhala Shop (p65)

Taxi

Call ahead for pickups from the following companies:

D&E Taxi (📞329-4279; 🕐6am-9pm)

Laura's Taxi (📞326-5466; www.luanalimo.com; 🕐5am-10pm)

AROUND KAILUA-KONA
Keauhou Resort Area

With wide thoroughfares and well-groomed landscapes, Keauhou feels like an upscale suburb: easy, pleasant and bland. Like most suburbs, there's no town center but there is a shopping mall. Rather, it is a collection of destinations: Keauhou Harbor for boat tours, Kahalu'u Beach for snorkeling and surfing, resorts and condos for sleeping, a farmers market and good restaurants, and a significant ancient Hawaiian settlement.

 Beaches

KAHALU'U BEACH PARK   Beach

Whether young or old, triathlete or couch potato, everyone appreciates Kahalu'u, the island's best easy-access **snorkeling** spot that also boasts offshore **surf breaks**. Protected by an ancient breakwater called Paokamenehune (which, according to legend, was built by the *menehune*, or 'little people'), the bay is pleasantly calm and shallow. You're guaranteed to see tropical fish and *honu* (green sea turtle) without even trying.

That said, Kahalu'u is too popular for its own good. Snorkelers can literally bump into one another. The salt-and-pepper beach (composed of lava and coral sand) is a mass of humanity, which you may find convivial or nauseating, depending. Due to its popularity, treading lightly is important; check out the educational efforts of the **ReefTeach Program** (www.kohalacenter.org/blog).

When the surf's up (and it can rage here), local surfers challenge the offshore waves, but they're too much for

beginners. Kahalu'u can harbor strong rip currents that pull in the northward direction off the rocks near St Peter's Church. The lifeguard-staffed park is well equipped with showers, restrooms, picnic tables and grills.

 Sights & Activities

A *pahoehoe* (smooth lava) rock shelf in front of the Outrigger Keauhou Beach Resort contains scads of tide pools. Here you'll see sea urchins, small tropical fish and, at high tide, green sea turtles.

ST PETER'S CHURCH   Church

An ever-popular setting for weddings, the picturesque Little Blue Church practically sits on the water. Made of clapboard and a corrugated-tin roof in the 1880s, the church was moved from White Sands Beach to its current site in 1912. This site was once an ancient Hawaiian temple, Ku'emanu Heiau. Hawaiian royalty, who surfed at the northern end of Kahalu'u Bay, paid their respects at the church before hitting the waves.

To get here, stop on the *makai* (seaward) side of Ali'i Dr, just north of the 5-mile marker.

ANCIENT HAWAIIAN SITES & TIDE POOLS   Historical Site

(Outrigger Keauhou Beach Resort, 78-6740 Ali'i Dr) On the resort grounds just south of Kahalu'u Beach Park, ancient Hawaiian sites and tide pools still remain along an easy-to-follow path. Ask at the resort's front desk for a map.

At the north end are the ruins of **Kapuanoni**, a fishing heiau (temple), and the reconstructed summer beach house of King Kalakaua next to a spring-fed pond that served as a royal bath. To the south are two major heiau. The first, **Hapaiali'i Heiau**, was built 600 years ago and in 2007 was completely restored by dry-stack masonry experts into a 15,000-sq-ft platform. Next to Hapaiali'i is the even larger **Ke'eku Heiau**, also recently restored. Legends say that Ke'eku was a *luakini* (temple of human sacrifice); most famously, a Maui chief who

Keauhou

tried to invade the Big Island was sacrificed here, and his grieving dogs still guard the site. Nearby **petroglyphs**, visible only at low tide, tell this story.

TOP **KEAUHOU FARMERS**
CHOICE **MARKET**   Market ·
(www.keauhoufarmersmarket.com; Keauhou Shopping Center, cnr Ali'i Dr & Kamehameha III Rd; ⊘8am-noon Sat) Buy fresh! Buy local! That's the apt slogan for this farmers

market where the produce is all Big Island grown. Find seasonal fruits and veggies, coffee, homemade preserves and baked goods, orchids and free-range eggs as well as free samples and live music. Unlike the touristy Kailua-Kona farmers markets selling knickknacks from who-knows-where, this neighborly event focuses on small-scale farmers and their fantastic bounty.

HO'OLA SPA   Spa
(☎930-4848; Sheraton Keauhou Bay Resort & Spa, 78-128 Ehukai St; 50min massage $120, 50min facial $125; ⏰8am-8pm) Although there are ritzier spas in South Kohala and North Kona, the Sheraton's 3200-sq-ft facility offers the best resort–spa experience in the Kailua-Kona vicinity. The menu of massages, facials and body wraps is rather predictable, but treatments are all well done. The stunning setting, overlooking crashing waves and lava rock, never lets you forget where you are.

KEAUHOU BAY & PIER   Landmark
Many tour cruises (see p43) launch from the small pier at this protected bay. While not a destination in itself, the small beach, picnic tables and sand volleyball courts bring locals out on their lunch hour. Snorkeling is possible in the calm bay, too. A local outrigger canoe club is headquartered here, and you can watch them practicing in the late afternoon.

Against the hillside, just south of the dive shacks, a stone marks the site where Kamehameha III was born in 1814. The young prince is said to have been stillborn and brought back to life by a visiting *kahuna* (priest).

To get here, turn *makai* (seaward) off Ali'i Dr onto Kamehameha III Rd. Restrooms and showers are available.

FREE Keauhou Kahalu'u Heritage Center   Heritage Center
(Keauhou Shopping Center, cnr Ali'i Dr & Kamehameha III Rd; ⏰10am-5pm) To learn more about the restoration of Keauhou's heiau, visit the this center, where displays and videos

DISCOVER KAILUA-KONA KEAUHOU RESORT AREA

also describe *holua* (ancient Hawaiian sport of sledding).

 Courses & Tours

OUTRIGGER KEAUHOU BEACH
RESORT   Cultural Courses & Tours
(☎ cultural programs 324-2540; www.
keauhoubeachresort.com, click on the Dining/
Activities tab) Intriguing Hawaiian language, hula and lei-making classes are
held weekdays from 8am to 3pm on the
grounds of the Outrigger Keauhou Beach
Resort as part of the resort's **Cultural
Program**. Ukulele and chant classes
are also on offer. Guided **daytime tours**
(adult/child 8-12 incl lunch $60/30) of the
resort's historical and cultural sites are
available, while the **evening tour** (adult/
child 8-12 incl dinner $85/45) highlights tradi-
tional navigating known as wayfaring.

At 8am every Tuesday, Outrigger
conducts a free one-hour cultural tour of
its grounds, including the restored heiau.

ORIGINAL HAWAIIAN
CHOCOLATE FACTORY   Tour
(☎ 322-2626, 888-447-2626; www.ohcf.us;
adult/child under 12 $10/free; ☉ 9am Wed,
9:30am Fri) A must for chocolate fans are
these exclusive one-hour tours detail-
ing how the *only* Hawaiian chocolate is
grown, harvested, processed and pack-
aged. Samples and sales available at
tour's end. The tour is great for kids. The
factory is located just under a mile inland
from Kailua-Kona; by appointment only.

If you're still craving quality chocolate
after the tour, head over to the Kailua
Candy Company where you can watch as
they hand-dip all their (splurge-worthy)
chocolates.

Keauhou Shopping
Center   Cultural Events
(www.keauhoushoppingcenter.com; cnr Ali'i Dr &
Kamehameha III Rd) The shopping center hosts
lively **cultural events** including a **ukulele jam
session** (☉ 6-8pm Wed, BYO ukulele) and a

hula show (🕑6pm Fri). Check the website for other classes and activities.

Kona Surf School   Surf Lessons
(☎217-5329; www.konasurfschool.com; 78-6685 Ali'i Dr; board rental day/week $25/99, surf lessons $100-150; 🕑8:30am-5pm) Just north of Kahalu'u Bay, offers board rentals and lessons daily (reservations required), including stand up paddle surfing ($75).

Festivals & Events

KONA CHOCOLATE FESTIVAL   Festival
(☎987-8722; www.konachocolatefestival.com; Sheraton Keauhou Bay Resort, 78-128 Ehukai St; admission advance booking/day of event $40/50) Indulge your sweet tooth at this three-day event, held in late March, which culminates in a gala evening of chocolate masterpieces by top Big Island chefs. Proceeds go to nonprofits such as Na'alehu Theater, an arts and education organization for kids.

Sleeping

Avoid rack rates at the hotels and resorts by advance booking online.

TOP CHOICE KONA TIKI HOTEL   Hotel $
(☎329-1425; www.konatiki.com; 75-5968 Ali'i Dr; r incl breakfast $85-100, with kitchenette $113; P🚳🌐) On a budget? You can still afford oceanfront units at the cozy Kona Tiki, a well-kept 15-unit complex. Rooms are basic (sans TV, phone and air-con) but clean, with fridge, lanai and fantastic oceanfront views. No credit cards.

TOP CHOICE HALE KONA KAI   Condo $$
(☎329-6402, 800-421-3696; www.halekonakai-hkk.com; 75-5870 Kahakai Rd; 1br $140-185; P❄🌐🚳) All rooms overlook crashing surf at this well-managed, oceanfront complex. The 22 units vary in style, but are all renovated and include separate living room, full kitchen and lanai overlooking the water. Ideally located off Ali'i Dr's main commercial stretch.

TOP CHOICE ROYAL SEA-CLIFF RESORT   Condo $$
(☎329-8021, 800-688-7444; www.outrigger.com; 75-6040 Ali'i Dr; studios $130, 1br $150-195, 2br $165-200; P❄@🌐🚳) The Outrigger resort runs the condo side of this seven-floor time-share complex like an upscale hotel, giving you the best of both worlds. Immaculate units are generously sized and uniformly appointed with pretty furniture and lots of amenities – well-stocked kitchens, washers and dryers, sauna and two oceanfront pools. You can't go wrong. Discounts online and off season.

CASA DE EMDEKO   Condo $$
(☎329-2160; www.casadeemdeko.org; 75-6082 Ali'i Dr; 1br & 2br from $95-135; ❄🚳) With Spanish-tile roofs, white stucco, immaculate gardens and two pools, this vacation rental complex is stylish and restful. Units are overall up-to-date, well-cared for and nicely priced. The off-highway location means no noise except wind, surf and tinkling chimes.

KONA MAGIC SANDS RESORT   Condo $$
(☎329-3333, 800-244-4752; www.konahawaii.com/ms.htm; 77-6452 Ali'i Dr; studio units $125-160; P❄🚳) Large studios offer oceanfront lanai, but 2nd- and especially 3rd-floor units are best. With White Sands Beach adjacent to the south, the location is perfect for beach-goers. The all-concrete building keeps out noise and heat. Hawaii Resort Management manages about 15 of 37 total units.

OUTRIGGER KEAUHOU BEACH RESORT   Hotel $$
(☎322-3441, reservations 866-326-6803; www.keauhoubeachresort.com; 78-6740 Ali'i Dr; r $140-230; P❄@🌐🚳) Location, location, location. This airy hotel is surrounded by Kahalu'u Beach to the north and tide pools all around. Oceanfront rooms literally overlook the water, where green sea turtles often appear. While not posh, the hotel was renovated in 2008 and has a pleasant, open-air design amid historically significant grounds.

Sushi platter, Kenichi Pacific

GREG ELMS / LONELY PLANET IMAGES ©

KONA REEF Condo **$$$**

(📞329-2959, 800-367-5004; www.kona reef.com; 75-5888 Ali'i Dr; 1br $260-350, 2br $425-520; P ❄ @ 🛜 🏊) The condos are spacious and well kept, but the complex itself is boring – dated, nondescript, lacking greenery and in need of a makeover. It's a better deal with an extended-stay or internet discount.

SHERATON KEAUHOU BAY
RESORT & SPA Resort **$$$**

(📞930-4900, 866-716-8109; www.sheraton keauhou.com; 78-128 'Ehukai St; r $350-460; ❄ @ 🛜 🏊 ♿) The only true 'resort' in the Kailua-Kona area, the Sheraton boasts a sleek modern design, upscale spa, massive pool with spiral slide, fine dining and over 500 rooms, but unfortunately no beach. Despite the grand atmosphere, the resort caters to kids, with a *keiki* center including foosball, PlayStation, basketball, ping-pong and movie theater. Internet rates are surprisingly affordable. Thumbs down, though, for the $16 per night mandatory resort fee (covering parking, wi-fi and other amenities), which is charged at check out.

OUTRIGGER KANALOA
AT KONA Condo **$$$**

(📞322-9625, reservations 866-733-0361; www.outriggerkanaloaatkonacondo.com; 78-261 Manukai St; 1br $295-365, 2br $325-499; P ❄ @ 🛜 🏊) This gated, townhouse-style condo feels exclusive, safe and private, sitting on an oceanfront lava ledge. Units are huge (one-bedroom units average 1200 sq ft to 1300 sq ft); two-bedroom units include two full bathrooms. With three pools, night-lit tennis courts and an adjacent golf course, you can practically stay put. Of the 166 units, Outrigger manages 84.

 Eating

TOP CHOICE **KENICHI**
PACIFIC Pacific Rim, Sushi **$$**

(📞322-6400; www.restauranteur.com/kenichi; Keauhou Shopping Center; sushi $5.50-10, mains $26-33; ⏰11:30am-1:30pm Tue-Fri, dinner from 5pm daily) Ignore the mall setting. Just savor the impeccable Pacific Rim fusion cuisine, finally done right. Memorable mains include subtly smoky bamboo salmon, miso pan-seared mahimahi, and

61

macadamia-crusted lamb with taro risotto. Sushi cuts are fresh and generous, while the molten chocolate cake is worth the splurge. Don't miss happy hour (from 4:30pm to 6:30pm), with half-price sushi rolls and drink specials.

PEABERRY & GALETTE   Cafe   **$**
(322-6020; www.peaberryandgalette. com; Keauhou Shopping Center; crepes $8-14; 7am-7pm Mon-Thu, to 8pm Fri & Sat, 8am-6pm Sun) With its Illy espresso, sleek decor and Euro-techno tunes, this cafe strives hard for uber-coolness. Never you mind. The kitchen serves delectable sweet and savory gourmet crepes, plus satisfying salads.

KAMA'AINA TERRACE   Hawaii Regional   **$$**
(322-3441; Outrigger Keauhou Beach Resort, 78-6740 Ali'i Dr; 6:30-10:30am & 5:30-9pm) Breakfast or *pupu* just go down better when you can see, smell and hear the ocean like here, at the Outrigger's oceanfront restaurant. The Aloha all-you-can-eat **buffet** (adult/child 6-12 $26/13; 11am-1pm), hosted every third Sunday, is an extravaganza of traditional Hawaiian dishes accompanied by fine Hawaiian music.

For quick, economical groceries and takeout, try the following:

Habaneros   Mexican   **$**
(324-4688; Keauhou Shopping Center; à la carte $3-7, plates $7-8; 9am-9pm Mon-Sat) Passable Mexican food.

KTA Super Stores   Grocery
(322-2311; Keauhou Shopping Center; 7am-10pm) Pharmacy inside.

🍸 Drinking & Entertainment

VERANDAH LOUNGE   Bar
(322-3441; Outrigger Keauhou Beach Resort, 78-6740 Ali'i Dr; 11am-9pm Sun-Thu, to 10pm Fri & Sat) Chill out at the wraparound bar with a drink in hand and waves crashing. The scene and crowd are sedate and mature. Live Hawaiian music sets the tone from 6:30pm to 9:30pm Friday and Saturday.

FIRENESIA   Luau
(326-4969; www.firenesia.com; Sheraton Keauhou Bay Resort, 78-128 'Ehukai St; adult/child 5-12 $80/50; 4:30pm Mon) The Sheraton luau (another Island Breeze production) is a fiery hero narrative weaving together several Polynesian tales and themes. The buffet (including ahi *poke,* Waimea mixed greens, seared mahimahi and roasted suckling pig) is surprisingly good.

Regal Cinemas Keauhou   Cinema
(324-0172; Keauhou Shopping Center, cnr Ali'i Dr & Kamehameha III Rd) Hollywood flicks fill seven screens. Matinee and Tuesday discounts.

ℹ Information

The following shops and other essentials are at the **Keauhou Shopping Center** (www. keauhoushoppingcenter.com; cnr Ali'i Dr & Kamehameha III Rd):

Bank of Hawaii (322-3280; 9am-6pm Mon-Fri, to 2pm Sat & Sun) With 24-hour ATM.

Keauhou Urgent Care Center (322-2544; 9am-7pm) Treatment for minor emergencies and illness. Walk-ins accepted.

Kona Stories (324-0350; www.konastories. com; 10am-7pm Mon-Fri, to 8pm Sat, to 5pm Sun) Good, independent bookstore with fun events for kids and adults.

Longs Drugs (322-5122; 8am-9pm Mon-Sat, to 6pm Sun)

Post office (322-7070; 9am-4pm Mon-Fri, 10am-3pm Sat)

ℹ Getting Around

Honu Express (fare $1; 9am-8pm) runs between Keauhou Shopping Center and Kailua Pier in Kailua-Kona, stopping at the Keauhou resorts, White Sand Beach and elsewhere. It makes half a dozen trips into downtown Kailua-Kona. Anyone can ride; you can pick up a schedule at the shopping center or download it at www. keauhoushoppingcenter.com.

Holualoa
POP 7093

Everyone should visit Holualoa, a diminutive coffee-farming village 1400ft above Kailua-Kona. The retro buildings, tight-knit community and slow pace preserve old Hawaii alongside the modern shops and art galleries. At this elevation, the climate is cooler and wetter, while coastal views are magnificent. Most businesses are closed on Sunday and Monday.

From Kailua-Kona, turn *mauka* (inland) on Hualalai Rd. The entire town is lined up along the Mamalahoa Hwy, just north of the Hualalai Rd intersection. Parking is easy most of the time, but terrible during popular festivals and events.

 **Sights & Activities**

Holualoa is a tiny village but don't underestimate the quality of its artists. Along Mamalahoa Hwy you'll find legitimate, internationally known, highly commissioned artists creating art beyond the stereotypical tropical motifs. Most galleries are open from 10am to 4pm, Tuesday to Saturday.

Standouts include the following:

IPU HALE GALLERY   Gallery
(☎ 322-9069; www.ipuguy.com) Rare collection of magnificent *ipu* (gourds) decoratively carved and dyed using an ancient Hawaiian method unique to Ni'ihau island. Owner Michael Harburg learned the technique in 1997 and is one of the island's only remaining practitioners.

HOLUALOA UKULELE GALLERY   Gallery
(☎ 324-4100; www.konaweb.com/ukegallery/index.html) Owner and artisan Sam Rosen displays beautifully handcrafted ukulele (which cost around $450 to $950) in a supercool, historic post office. Rosen also runs 10-day and 10-week ukulele-making workshops. Stop by to listen to a *kanikapila* (jam session) on Wednesday evenings (from 6pm to 8:30pm).

DONKEY MILL ART CENTER   Gallery
(☎ 322-3362; www.donkeymillartcenter.org; 78-6670 Hwy 180; admission free; ☺10am-4pm Tue-Sat) The Holualoa Foundation for Arts & Culture established this community-minded art center in 2002. Open to visitors are free exhibits, plus lectures and workshops taught by recognized national

Upcountry Coffee Tasting

Gourmet coffee has long gone mainstream, and many farms have established visitor centers, where they give free tours and samples. See www.konacoffeefest.com/drivingtour for a list.

Mountain Thunder Coffee Plantation (☎325-2136, 888-414-5662; www.mountainthunder.com; 73-1944 Hao St; ☺9am-4pm Mon-Sat) Established in 1998, this award-winning organic farm is located in lush Kaloko Mauka, about 15 minutes from Kailua-Kona. Free 20-minute tours are detailed (and wheelchair accessible), but for a real in-depth look at Kona coffee, try the VIP Tours (per person $65 to $135, lunch extra; reserve ahead) or become Roast Master for a Day (per person $199), and you roast 5lb of your own beans.

Holualoa Kona Coffee Company (☎877-322-9937, 800-334-0348; www.konalea.com; 77-6261 Mamalahoa Hwy; ☺8am-4pm Mon-Fri) The Kona Le'a Plantation does not use pesticides or herbicides on its beautiful organic farm; the tours are excellent.

Hula Daddy Kona Coffee (☎327-9744; www.huladaddy.com; 74-4944 Hwy 180; ☺10am-2pm Tue-Sat) The attractive tasting room is the place for cupping seminars.

Kona Blue Sky Coffee (☎877-322-1700; www.konablueskycoffee.com; 76-973A Hualalai Rd; ☺9am-3:30pm Mon-Sat) In Holualoa village, this estate's tour includes the traditional open-air drying racks and a video; it has a nice gift shop.

Detour:
Dr Do-A-Lot

Dr Dolittle talked to the animals. Dr Ann Goody communes with them, fixes their broken bones and psyches, coaxes them back into their natural behavior and sets them free. Or not – some rescued and exotic animals just can't cut it in the wild. That's when they become residents of the **Three Ring Ranch Exotic Animal Sanctuary** (www.threeringranch.org) on five lovely upcountry acres just a short drive from downtown Kailua-Kona.

Licensed by the US Department of Agriculture and accredited by the American Association of Sanctuaries (the only sanctuary in the state and one of only 33 nationally with this distinction), Three Ring currently hosts South African–crowned cranes, lesser flamingos, David and Goliath (a pair of gigantic African spur-thigh tortoises) and native endangered species such as the Hawaiian owl. Like the very best mentors, healers and caretakers, it's clear Dr Goody doesn't play favorites, but zebra Zoe is something special; rescued from the failed Moloka'i Ranch Safari Park, Zoe has amelanosis, meaning her stripes are the color of Hapuna Beach sand and her eyes the color of the water.

Dr Goody – who has been struck by lightning, tossed by a shark and survived breast cancer – is as good with people as she is with animals. This, along with the unflagging support of her husband and business partner Dr Norm Goody, has led to enormously successful educational initiatives, including an after-school program, a resident intern program and a residency placement program. The sanctuary's primary commitment is to the animals so its two-hour **tours** (suggested donation $35; ⏲11am) are by prior arrangement only.

and international artists. The center's building, constructed in 1953, was once a coffee mill with a donkey painted on its roof, hence the name. It's 3 miles south of the village center.

Studio 7 Gallery — Gallery
(☎324-1335) This serene, museum-like gallery features prominent artist and owner Hiroki Morinoue's watercolor, oil, woodblock and sculpture pieces. Setsuko, his wife, is an accomplished potter and the gallery's director.

Dovetail — Gallery
(☎322-4046; www.dovetailgallery.net) Showcases elegant work by local artist and custom-furniture designer Gerald Ben.

Malama I Ka Ola Holistic Health Center — Health Center
(☎324-6644; 76-5914 Mamalahoa Hwy) This health center offers yoga and pilates classes,

as well as massage, acupuncture and other alternative skin and healthcare treatments.

Festivals & Events

Coffee & Art Stroll — Event
During November's Kona Coffee Cultural Festival (p46), Holualoa hosts a super-popular, day-long block party.

Summer Farmfest & Ukulele Jam — Festival
Offers a bounty of local produce and music; held each June.

Music & Light Festival — Festival
A wonderful Christmas celebration held in December. For more information, see www.holualoahawaii.com.

Sleeping

TOP CHOICE **HOLUALOA INN** Inn $$$

(📞324-1121, 800-392-1812; www.
holualoainn.com; 76-5932 Hwy 180; r $260-350,
ste $280-375; 🅿 📶 ⛵) Hands-down, this is
one of the island's classiest, most romantic
properties. From the gleaming eucalyptus
floors to the unwoven *lauhala* (hala leaf)
walls and river-rock showers, serene beau-
ty and comfort shine in every detail; several
gorgeous public rooms graced with tasteful
Asian art and exquisite carved furniture
segue seamlessly into the outdoor gardens
and pool. It's good that the rooftop gazebo
surveys the world since not all six rooms
have ocean views. All in all, it makes a
peaceful, intimate retreat. No TVs, phones,
or children under 13. There's a kitchenette
for guest use. Rates include breakfast.

TOP CHOICE **Lilikoi Inn** Inn $$

(📞333-5539; www.lilikoiinn.com; r incl
breakfast $110-135; 📶) You're going to love the
four rooms here, each with a private entrance,
and access to hot tub, guest laundry, kitchen
and lanai. Breakfasts are restaurant-worthy.

Orchid Inn Inn $$

(📞324-0252; www.theorchidinn.com; 76-5893A
Old Government Rd; d $169; @ 📶) One exotic
African suite with a handsome bed angled for a
stupendous ocean view.

Kona Hotel Hostel $

(📞324-1155; Hwy 180; with shared bathroom s
$30, d $35-40) This boarding house (c 1926) falls
into the 'only if absolutely necessary' category.
It's cheap and you get what you pay for: surly
service and dirty communal bathrooms.

 Eating

TOP CHOICE **HOLUAKOA GARDENS
& CAFÉ** Cafe $$

(📞322-2233; Hwy 180; brunch $11-15, dinner
$22-32; 🕐10am-2:30pm Tue-Fri, 9am-2:30pm
Sat & Sun, dinner 5:30-8:30pm Tue-Sat) This

Leaves of Hala

Hawaiians wove the dried *lau*
(leaves) of the *hala* (pandanus) tree
into floor mats, hats, baskets, fans
and other household items. Strong
and flexible, *lauhala* is surprisingly
hardy and long-lasting. Today,
most *lauhala* items sold in Hawaii
are actually mass-produced in the
Philippines and sold cheaply to
unwitting tourists. But, in Holualoa,
Kimura Lauhala Shop (📞324-0053;
cnr Hualalai Rd & Mamalahoa Hwy; 🕐9am-
5pm Mon-Fri, to 4pm Sat), now run by the
Kimura family's fourth generation,
sells high-quality, genuine Hawaiian
lauhala crafts. Originally, the family
purchased *lauhala* items from
Hawaiian weavers to sell at the
family's general store, but during the
Great Depression, a family member
learned the craft. Now, local weavers
supply the shop with a variety of
handmade souvenir and gift items,
from traditional hats to zipper
purses and signature lined totes.

organic, slow food restaurant with
peaceful gardens and ponds has a sea-
sonally adapted menu featuring creative
dishes like homemade gnocchi with
morels, leeks and edamame (boiled soy-
beans), and grilled ahi with roasted fig
and ginger fried-rice dishes. At brunch,
try the rocking frittata. Service is casual;
book ahead for dinner. For early risers,
the **cafe** (🕐6:30am-3pm Mon-Fri, 8am-3pm
Sat & Sun) does good java and pastries.

As one of Hawai'i's most dedicated
establishments to supporting local
farmers, it's no surprise there's a
Saturday Farmers Market (🕐9am-noon
Sat) hosted at the gardens.